Advance review praise for *This Has Happened*

"[A] haunting memoir. . . . In spare, beautifully translated language, Sonnino details her life in Genoa. . . . The author's account of the last night [the Sonnino family] spent together is eloquent. . . . [A] searing testimony."

—*Publishers Weekly* (Starred Review)

"A moving account of a family caught up in the Shoah. . . . Four illuminating essays bookend this memoir. Denby acknowledges the 'tinge of irritation and guilt' people often feel upon publication of a Holocaust memoir, then brilliantly demonstrates why this one is necessary. . . . His arresting foreword is followed by a helpful sketch of the historical background from [. . .] Goldstein, who also crafted this wonderful English translation. An epilogue by Italian journalist Giacomo Papi describes how the manuscript came to light, and novelist Mary Doria Russell's provocative afterword explains why Italian Jews fared relatively better than their brethren in the rest of Europe. An important contribution to Holocaust literature."

—*Kirkus* (Starred Review)

This Has Happened

An Italian Family in Auschwitz

Piera Sonnino

Translated by
Ann Goldstein

Foreword by
David Denby

Epilogue by
Giacomo Papi

Afterword by
Mary Doria Russell

palgrave
macmillan

THIS HAS HAPPENED
© 2004, Gruppo Editoriale il Saggiatore
English-language edition copyright © 2006 Palgrave
Macmillan

First published in English in 2006 by
PALGRAVE MACMILLAN™
175 Fifth Avenue, New York, N.Y. 10010 and
Houndmills, Basingstoke, Hampshire, England RG21 6XS
Companies and representatives throughout the world.

First published in Italy as *Questo è stato* by Gruppo
Editoriale il Saggiatore

PALGRAVE MACMILLAN is the global academic imprint of
the Palgrave Macmillan division of St. Martin's Press, LLC
and of Palgrave Macmillan Ltd. Macmillan® is a registered
trademark in the United States, United Kingdom and other
countries. Palgrave is a registered trademark in the
European Union and other countries.

ISBN-13: 978–1–4039–7508–9
ISBN-10: 1–4039–7508–6

Library of Congress Cataloging-in-Publication Data

Sonnino, Piera, 1922–1999.
   [Questo è stato. English]
   This has happened : an Italian family in Auschwitz / by
Piera Sonnino ; translated by Ann Goldstein.
     p. cm.
   ISBN 1–4039–7508–6 (alk. paper)
    1. Sonnino, Piera, 1922–1999. 2. Jews—Italy—
Biography. 3. Holocaust, Jewish (1939–1945)—Italy—
Personal narratives. I. Title.

DS135.I9S66713 2006
940.53'18092—dc22   2006044296

A catalogue record of the book is available from the British
Library.

Design by Newgen Imaging Systems, Ltd., Chennai, India

First edition: November 2006

10 9 8 7 6 5 4 3 2 1

Printed in the United States of America.

Contents

Photo section appears after page 109

Foreword

David Denby

DAVID DENBY has been a film critic and staff writer for *The New Yorker* since 1998. In the past, he has been film critic of *The Atlantic*, *The Boston Phoenix*, and *New York* magazine. His essays on literature and culture have appeared in *The New Republic* and *The New York Review of Books*. He has written two books, *Great Books* and *American Sucker*.

A manuscript appears, seemingly out of nowhere, composed by a woman one has never heard of. The manuscript is devoted to the most terrible experience of the twentieth century: when she was young, the woman, Piera Sonnino, lost her entire family in the Nazi death camps. The most terrible experience, yet one also thinks—with a tinge of irritation and guilt—an experience familiar to us in certain ways. Can one read the manuscript? Must one? Don't we have works by Elie Wiesel and Primo Levi and many other skilled and eloquent writers devoted to the catastrophe? In 1960, almost forty years before her death, Piera Sonnino wrote down the events of her life during the war solely for the benefit of her daughters, without thought of publication.* Yet after her death, the work was published; now it is a text, a book, a Holocaust memoir—one of many. And so we are stuck: although no one may presume to judge the quality of the experience undergone by a survivor, judging the quality of the survivor's writing is an inescapable act. That response, however, makes many of us uneasy. Dreading a merely "literary" relationship with Sonnino's work, one thinks before reading it that perhaps the manuscript should be turned over to historians. It is a valuable document—isn't that enough? After all, is there anything new to be said about the death camps, about Auschwitz?

The story begins a little stiffly, with a formal introduction to the eight members of a Genoese Jewish family—father, mother, three brothers, three sisters—

---

* See the translator's introduction and the epilogue by the Italian journalist Giacomo Papi for further details of Sonnino's life and the history of her memoir.

as the family existed before the Second World War. The introduction, offered without physical detail, without flesh, with only a touch of anecdote—Piera's mother would begin playing popular songs at the piano only to fall into a classical sonata—comes off as exceptionally dignified and a little remote. They are an Italian Jewish family as defined by the occupations of each member and the social position of the family as a whole. To outsiders, they may have seemed haughty. The girls were too proud to invite anyone to their house, since the guests would have noticed, as Piera implies, the shabbiness of the furniture. A middle-class family, then, holding onto gentility; a group of people shy, reserved, incurious, conventionally refined, and perhaps a little embarrassed by the business occupations that social circumstances force them to take. Piera makes it clear that she and her brothers and sisters had no romantic lives to speak of, no passions, no obsessional drives or habits, that they defined themselves as a family unit with a collective destiny, not as a group of individuals seeking self-realization and happiness.

In 1938, the Fascist government promulgated the racial laws that severely restricted their rights as citizens. For years, dignity had been the family's protective shield; they wanted to be still, unobtrusive; they wanted not to be noticed. But dignity, with its reflexive habits of disconnection and obliviousness, now became a serious danger as well; the family was not in the closest touch with the reality closing in on them. Piera Sonnino understands this, of course, better than any of us, and she says something very interesting about it: "The official optimism of the [Fascist] regime did not admit or tolerate economic catastrophe. We who were not infected by Fascism saw clearly the unbridgeable gap between reality and official optimism, but I think this, in the end, even if we were unconscious of it, in some way legitimized what we considered dignity and decorum." This is a considerable insight; it suggests how thoroughly a dictatorial government can affect the gentler mental habits of its citizens as well as their physical behavior. If one could have served as Sonnino's editor, one would have asked her to delve into the matter and explain it in greater detail. But she does not explain, and the story sweeps on: the racial laws are enacted; the family withdraws even further into its fortress; the disaster approaches. As the Mussolini government collapses in 1943, and the Nazis occupy Italy and round up Jews for deportation, Sonnino and her family leave Genoa and begin the year of hiding and flight that will end, after they are denounced and captured, in the cattle cars heading to Poland.

But now a surprise: as the narrative moves toward tragedy, the style changes, too, and one begins to understand that the stiffness of the opening pages was not a compositional weakness but the result of a writer's conscious decision or natural instinct. In either case, it must be understood as the work of a *writer,* not of an amateur struggling to launch a narrative. Each sentence now seems a completed unit of meaning, sufficient in its terse bareness as the absolute expression of what Sonnino needs to convey: At the time, the family understood so much, and nothing more. The family was both ennobled and hampered by its commitment to propriety and silence, and Sonnino's writing, by what it omits, replicates the strengths and limitations of the family's way of thinking.

On the run, however, the Sonninos cannot cling to the same illusions and defenses, and, as physical hardship and cruelty overwhelm them, the narrative picks up speed and an implacable urgency. Sonnino reveals a talent for suggestive anecdote, as in the story of her brother Roberto's meeting with a peasant who pointedly tells him that "a family of Jews was hiding in the neighborhood," making it dangerous for everyone. After the Sonninos are deported, the episode of the women rushing from the train to bring water back to the men is conveyed in no more than a few words, and with the hallucinated clarity of a soundless episode in a film. As the family, its numbers diminishing, moves through the stages of hell—from Auschwitz, to Belsen, to Braunschweig, to Bendorf—the writing grows progressively more tactile and physical, the mental states more sharply noted, even in their fragments and incomprehensions, and the emotions more extreme, at times reaching levels of terror and horrified revulsion checked only by a grim desire to tell everything.

On only one occasion, re-creating the family's last night together, does Sonnino refuse to write: "Whatever I could say of that time, it wouldn't make sense translated into words; it would be a thin shadow of that reality. I would be stealing it from myself, from what is mine, desperately mine alone." But she knows the rest is not hers alone. It must be spoken. The mud at Auschwitz "didn't seem like earth and water: but something organic that had decomposed, putrefied flesh that has turned liquid." In Braunschweig, Piera's younger sister Bice—the only other family member still alive—"was visibly losing her strength. Her eighteen years seemed to be contracted, almost crumpled, she was like a leaf torn, still green, from a tree, lying in the dust in the sun. She was becoming a creature without age, pale with that papery white pallor of the 'subhumans.'" Bice dies and is dumped on a bench outside the camp latrine, where her body is slowly covered by snow; and then Piera, as if unable to look at any more, accidentally breaks her glasses. The combination of an insupportable memory and diminished sight brings coherent re-creation almost to a halt. Exhausted, half-starved, increasingly given to dangerous inattention and revery, she has lost everyone and may have been tempted to lose herself. At that point, syntax, imitating the near dissolution of consciousness, breaks down into tiny integers of notation. "A face. Frozen. I have slept on a dead woman. Again a void. Choruses of cries like a furious, wailing wind."

———

This memoir, among a great many other things, embodies the saddest of ironies: the Sonninos' unselfish devotion to one another, their determination to stick together as a family at all times, may have hastened their destruction. The older boys might have escaped into the mountains in northern Italy. But they did not escape; their mother wanted the family in one piece. And that irony, among many other things, makes this devotional family text a fresh contribution to Holocaust literature. Historians will note the details of deportation, the acts of both solidarity and betrayal by fellow Italians; psychologists will study the physical and moral condition of extremity and the responses to it, the structuring of observation and grief; literary critics will judge the appositeness of technique and expression. But readers with a family—that is to say, anyone who reads the memoir—cannot fail to be moved by the loving care the Sonninos offered to one another, and then by the separations and deaths, one by one.

Inevitably, we ask about Piera: Why did she survive? For if she was half dead in Braunschweig and Bendorf, the other half won out. The answer is that she was strong and also lucky; she didn't fall ill. And also, we think, she survived because she had this story to tell. As she was living it, thinking at the end only of her sister Bice's next breath, she was unconsciously storing up a purpose. When it was realized, the purpose seems not to have included publication; the old family reserve and pride reasserted itself in Piera's decision to keep the memoir a private matter. In this respect, she is akin to the aristocratic writers of the eighteenth and nineteenth century for whom self-expression and family enlightenment were enough, and publication an indignity to be avoided. But now we think—as she must have thought, too—that writing completed the miracle of survival.

Surviving, Piera writes the anguished phrase, "I, alone of my entire family, returned to life" (a devastating echo of the Book of Job's "And I only am escaped alone to tell thee"). By saying that one reason she needed to survive was to write, I do not mean to set up a hierarchy of survivors—those who wrote and those who remained silent. The latter are no less blessed than the writers, but they have not been lucky enough to have achieved this late flowering of self, this willingness to tell, even if the willingness comprised no more than the desire that two daughters should know what happened to their long-dead grandparents, aunts, and uncles. As it happens, Piera Sonnino has written well, with a grip on narrative sequence, a sustained emotional tension and grandeur, a heartbreaking alternation of memory and desire that no professional writer could possibly condescend to. She is a true writer. A reader, shedding his distaste for a literary response, cannot help noticing that the death of Bice is so powerful, in part, because it is perfectly composed. And a reader who approached the "stiff" opening pages with skepticism also cannot fail to notice that the family habit of dignified composure is reasserted in a stern ethos of compositional rectitude. Piera Sonnino refuses to give way to hatred or denunciation. In this reluctance, she is like her great compatriot Primo Levi. Her words, like his, have a force beyond any denunciation.

Setting the Stage

A Brief Historical Background

Ann Goldstein

ANN GOLDSTEIN is an editor at *The New Yorker*. She has translated works by, among others, Pier Paolo Pasolini, Alessandro Baricco, Elena Ferrante, and Roberto Calasso, and is currently editing the *Complete Works of Primo Levi* in English. She has been the recipient of the PEN Renato Poggioli prize, a grant from the National Italian American Foundation, and a translation award from the Italian Ministry of Foreign Affairs.

B enito Mussolini and the Fascists came to power in 1922, and during the next few years Mussolini turned the government into a dictatorship. In the thirties, he sought to realize his imperial ambitions by invading Ethiopia; he sent troops to support Franco in the Spanish Civil War; and, eventually, he became allied with Hitler.

Unlike the Nazis, the Fascists did not include racism and anti-Semitism as a specific part of their program. However, between August and November 1938, Mussolini promulgated a series of racial laws. Under these laws, Jews were no longer permitted to teach in or to attend high schools and universities, and could not marry non-Jews. There were restrictions on the kinds of business they could engage in, and they were banned from the armed forces and the civil service. Foreign Jews were expelled.

The Italian Jewish community was one of the oldest in Europe; Jews had lived in Italy for some two thousand years. In the 1930s they numbered around 47,000, and were well integrated into Italian society, generally thinking of themselves as Italians rather than as Jews; they held government and university positions, and several thousand were even members of the Fascist Party. After the racial laws went into effect, although there was not the same sort of persecution as in Nazi Germany, life became difficult; for example, the Sonnino siblings had to find new jobs or leave their schools for special Jewish schools that were established.

In 1940 Italy entered the Second World War as Germany's ally, which meant declaring war on Britain and France and, the following year, on America and Russia. Starting in mid-1940, Genoa, as an important industrial and shipping center, was bombed by the Allies, and many families were evacuated. Sometime in 1941 or 1942 the Sonnino family left Genoa and went to live in Sampierdicanne, a section of the town of Chiavari, south of the city. (The memoir is not entirely clear about when, though Piera had evidently finished school by then and gone to work.) In June 1943 the Allies invaded Sicily and southern Italy and began slowly making their way north. Bombing intensified.

As the war went badly for the Italians on all fronts, Mussolini lost the confidence of his own party, and in July 1943, at a meeting of the Fascist Grand Council, he was removed from power by his colleagues and replaced by Marshal Pietro Badoglio, backed by King Victor Emmanuel III. While ostensibly maintaining ties with the Germans, Badoglio secretly negotiated a truce—essentially, a surrender—with the Allied forces. This agreement became public on September 8, and then, in fear of the Germans, he (and the King) fled south to Brindisi, leaving the country in chaos. The Allies were still far south of Rome, and the Germans immediately took possession of northern and central Italy, including Rome. They installed Mussolini as the head of a powerless puppet government in the north, known as the Republic of Salò. (The majority of Italian Jews lived in northern and central Italy.) The country became a battleground as the Allies fought their way north; in the occupied north, the Germans brutally repressed any resistance, military or civilian. The historian R. J. B. Bosworth points out that between September 1943 and the end of the summer of 1945 "as many Italians died as had perished in the campaigns from 1940–43 while Mussolini was still *duce* of a united nation, the majority, 200,000, being civilians." The army was in complete disarray. Many units simply scattered; some soldiers joined the Allies or the Germans; and 600,000 troops were disarmed by the Germans and interned or sent to labor camps in Germany.

With the German occupation, the situation of the Jews changed drastically: the Nazis began to round up and arrest Jews in many of the major cities under their control, including Venice, Turin, and Genoa. They were sent to internment or transit camps in Italy, and from there to the German extermination camps. Thus, after September 8, the Sonnino family could no longer live openly, if constrictedly, in Chiavari, but had to escape or find a place to hide. At this point, they went to the mountain village of Pietra di Rovegno. The mountains in this area, where the Sonninos stayed through the fall and into the winter of 1943–1944, were home to various partisan groups fighting a guerrilla war against the Germans and the Fascists; there had been opposition groups from the start of the Fascist dictatorship, but after September 8 the number of groups and their membership increased dramatically. As Sonnino notes, she and her family were unaware of these groups, although they were operating so close by.

It was an occupied country and a war zone: the Allied bombing was fierce, food was scarce, and people could barely help themselves, let alone one another. In the winter of 1944 the Sonnino family, discovered by the local *carabinieri** to be Jews, found no recourse but to return to Nazi-Fascist–controlled Genoa. The most severe roundups and deportations had taken place when the Nazis first took control of the city in the fall of 1943, but they

* The *carabinieri* are a military unit that has civil police duties.

continued to hunt down Jews and offered rewards to those who reported them. Yet the family managed to survive for nine months without discovery. Meanwhile, the progress of the Allies north was extremely slow; Rome was liberated in June 1944, Florence in August. In October, the Sonnino family was arrested and almost immediately sent in a convoy to Auschwitz.

Genoa was not freed until the following April. Mussolini, attempting to escape to Switzerland, was captured by partisans and killed on April 28, 1945. Germany surrendered to the Allies on May 2.

Altogether, about 7,500 Italian Jews were deported to the concentration camps, of whom only about six hundred survived.

This Has Happened

An Italian Family
in Auschwitz

Piera Sonnino

Translated from the Italian by Ann Goldstein

Genoa, July 20, 1960

My name is Piera Sonnino. I was born thirty-eight years ago in Portici, near Naples, the fourth of six children of my mother, Giorgina Milani, and my father, Ettore Sonnino. Their wedding, celebrated in a Jewish ceremony in Rome in 1910, was lavish, in keeping with the social position of both families, and the ceremony concluded with a concert in which a well-known soprano of the time took part. For my mother, deeply in love with the man who had become her husband, and for my father, their life together had an auspicious start.

Their first child was Paolo, who was followed by Roberto, Maria Luisa, me, Bice, and Giorgio. My father was a handsome man. In the only photograph of him that has survived, he is still young, and has the look of an elegant, turn-of-the-century gentleman, with a somewhat arrogant air. He was kind and generous, as the Neapolitans are. He came from a middle-class family—the Honorable Sidney Sonnino was a cousin of our grandfather*—and for his entire life, in spite of his physical decline and the atrocious humiliations he endured, he maintained, up until the final long night of Auschwitz, a natural refinement that instilled respect and obedience in us, his children. For many years the profession imposed on him by family tradition and—I believe—undertaken with many reservations, was that of a businessman, a shop manager or salesman, depending on the circumstances, and he pursued it with variable, and usually limited,

* Sonnino (1847–1922) was a politician who twice served as Prime Minister.

success. In the periods when luck was with him or when he managed to conclude a favorable deal, my father, with an almost childish enthusiasm, filled the house with all sorts of things that, no matter how superfluous, he thought might brighten the lives of his wife and children. Even before 1938, the year in which the racial laws took effect and the situation of our family, both human and social, fell apart, we spent many days of dignified poverty comforted by gramophones and the latest cameras. Needless to say, these testaments to better times disappeared quickly under the pressure of household necessities.

My mother was born in Rome. She had earned a teaching diploma and was also an excellent pianist. She declared that she was an enemy of popular music, but we, her children, sometimes managed to make her forget Bach and Haydn, and would lovingly coax her to sit at the piano and play the songs that were in fashion. It always happened that in the middle of some light melody the music would suddenly stop and the notes of a sonata would rise into the air. Mamma played with absorption, as if she were drawing those often melancholy passages from within herself, and not just from her memory. At a distance of many years, and with the experience that life has brought, I've found that the love I always felt for my mother has been transformed into reverence.

Today I can fully appreciate, and, if not always comprehend, at least imagine, what a complex and heavy burden she carried, what a sum of sorrows tortured her for years, before the end that awaited her. My mother did not have a greatly expansive nature, like the other members of my family; her rules were silence and control of one's own feelings. But I remember when these rules were broken by events, the day we were arrested, and our last, long night in the transit shed of Auschwitz: I recall the continuous, uninterrupted weeping of a woman in anguish.

Paolo had graduated in 1940 with a degree in business and economics. He had had to work to support himself during his studies, and, particularly after the promulgation of the racial laws, the jobs that he found were always temporary and poorly paid. His degree was the result of great sacrifices and a serious and tenacious character. I think that although Paolo was the oldest and enjoyed a longer period of tranquility than the rest of us, he died having had no experience of love. In our house certain subjects were forbidden, and love was among them, but if there had been hints about Paolo I would remember. Instead, in my memory he is totally absorbed, first by work and study and then by our common anxiety: the anxiety that denied to us, too, his brothers and sisters, youth and love and even the chance to dream of a future. For five years, starting in 1938, we lived in a time without a future, a dark present overhung by a confused and indistinct nightmare, which enveloped us after September 8, 1943.

At fifteen, my brother Roberto had to interrupt his studies and go to work. What my father earned was not, as usual, sufficient to provide even a modest living for our family, which from 1925 included eight people. Roberto's first contribution was two hundred *lire* a month. Roberto was a practical, cheerful youth who loved life. As, gradually, our father and mother were increasingly unable to react to the nightmare that pressed around us, he became if not the mainstay the one who, more than any of us, assumed the family responsibilities. It was Roberto who took initiatives that many times procured food for us or got us out of terrifying situations. He was anything but contemplative and, if he could have continued his studies, probably would not have had the same success as Paolo—though not, certainly, because he was less intelligent. He had the somewhat disorganized, capricious character of a man of good sense and many ideas.

Giorgio was the youngest. From the age of discretion, he grew up in the nightmare. He spent the last nine months of his existence shut up within the walls of the apartment on Via Montallegro, in the neighborhood of San Martino, where we had found lodging and refuge. For nine long months he was cut off from society and from life. He became nervous to an extreme degree, and during the aerial bombardments he suffered breakdowns that left him exhausted. We, his sisters, brought him books: he asked us continually for history books, in particular about the first *Risorgimento*.* He became profoundly knowledgeable about the lives of Mazzini and Garibaldi. In the last days he had begun to memorize a dictionary, and in the morning, when he came to help us in the kitchen, he would ask us the meaning of the most abstruse, least modern words he could

---

* A reference to the nineteenth-century nationalist movement that resulted in the unification of the separate countries of the Italian peninsula.

find, entertaining himself by embarrassing us. We gave him the opportunity to embark on long dissertations that originated in the need that he had, and that we understood, to feel, through his words, that he was alive. But these were rare moments of relaxation. Giorgio, minute by minute, day by day, lived nine months of terror. He was the first among us to enter the antechamber of death, and when death arrived he yielded without resistance.

Maria Luisa was the oldest sister. She was beautiful, and her character was similar in many ways to Roberto's. At Auschwitz and, later, when we were separated from our parents, in Belsen and Braunschweig, she was like a mother to Bice and me. Sometimes now, at a distance of fifteen years, when there is silence all around me, I seem to hear again her thin, hoarse voice rising in the barracks, as she sang for Bice and me, to keep alive in us the absurd hope of surviving. One evening, when we had just returned to the barracks in Braunschweig that we few Italian Jews shared with seven hundred Hungarian Jews, a supervisor came to read a list of those of us who were to be deported. Among them was Maria Luisa. Our sister lined up with the others whose names had been called. Bice and I thought that they were bound for an extra work shift, as often happened. Our sister wasn't even given time to say goodbye to us. We never saw her again.

Bice, of all of us, most resembled our mother, above all in her character. She was the second-youngest and still a child at Auschwitz, at Belsen, at Braunschweig. For four days her body lay abandoned on a wooden bench and in the end disappeared under the snow. My father, Ettore Sonnino, and my mother, Giorgina Milani, at the ages of seventy-four and fifty-eight, respectively, were killed in the gas chambers at Birkenau on October 28, 1944. Paolo, at the age of twenty-seven, and Roberto, at the age of twenty-six, were killed in November. Giorgio, at the age of nineteen, was killed a few days after his brothers. Maria Luisa was killed at Flossenburg on March 20, 1945, at the age of twenty-five. Bice was killed at Braunschweig on the night of January 15–16, 1945. She was twenty-one. The number that death imprinted on my arm, and that I still bear, is: A26699. In September 1950, after five years in rehabilitation centers and sanatoriums, I, alone of my entire family, returned to life.

The first signs of the nightmare reached us between 1934 and 1935. German Jews expelled from Nazi Germany were constantly arriving in Genoa, where we had lived since 1925, and the community helped them as much as it could, directing them for further aid to other Jewish families.

Their number increased to the point where we ended up having very little to share. These first victims of Nazi anti-Semitism, ragged and starving, entered our house as if ashamed, and thanked us effusively if we could give them anything. None of them spoke Italian, but many knew French, and in that language they tried to explain to us, in lowered voices, as if they were afraid of not being believed, what was happening in Germany. Jewish shops and homes attacked and destroyed, Jews severely beaten, killed—a blind, premeditated fury that was growing. The stories we heard seemed to belong to a world so distant from ours that it represented a different reality. We couldn't imagine that any neighbor of ours, any acquaintance, any of the thousands and thousands of strangers we encountered every day would be capable of entering our house, of attacking our father and mother, of harming us because we were Jews. We said these things to the Jewish refugees from Hitler's Germany and they shook their heads sadly. Nazism is a gangrene that will spread widely, they said. After 1935 the refugees abruptly ceased to arrive, and we thought that the situation had somehow become normal. Instead, the death struggle of the German Jews had begun and we were unaware of it, as we were unaware that those camps, where just nine years later our family would be exterminated, had begun operations.

The exodus of the Jews from Hitler's Germany had sowed in us suspicions and worries, however vague. Although we took no part in the common life of the community to which we belonged, and were aligned neither on one side nor the other of the barricade, the resemblance between Fascism and Nazism could not escape us, nor the steps that the two dictatorships were fatally taking toward one another. These sensations were still confused, and not yet conscious—presentiments that we, like our fellow Jews, repressed, because it is a particular characteristic of the Jews to believe that the desire to be ignored is transformed, precisely because it is a desire, into the reality of being ignored.

It was in these years that the financial situation of our family worsened. Papa and Mamma, after their marriage, had moved from Rome to Portici and then, in 1923, with the children who were already born—Paolo, Roberto, Maria Luisa, and I—to Milan. In Milan, Bice and Giorgio were born, and Giorgio was only a few months old when, after a new move, we settled in Genoa. My father had become the manager of a shop in Piazza Campetto, and that seemed to open up good prospects for the future. Three years later, however, with his usual bad luck, Papa had to resume the old, unprofitable profession of salesman. In 1935, as I said, Roberto abandoned his studies and went to work.

My memories of that period are not very pleasant. There were many days when we had nothing, in the literal sense of the word, to eat. Several times, the elderly lawyer Giuseppe Fontana, who treated us as his grandchildren and never could have imagined our situation, bought Maria Luisa, Bice, and me an ice cream when we met him in the gardens of Piazza Manin, which served as both lunch and dinner. We hid our poverty from strangers by every possible means. We all became expert at preventing anyone who didn't belong to our narrow family circle from coming to our house and noticing the gaps that appeared among the furniture and knickknacks. We girls were at the age when one likes to invite school friends home and be invited, in turn, to play, study, and spend time together. We couldn't aspire to any of these things but had, rather, to keep our relations with our classmates on a superficial level, learning to contain and repress any impulse of sympathy.

Today I no longer entirely understand such embarrassment or shame about our poverty, except in the context of the economic and social disaster that during those years befell numerous families in the lower and middle classes—those, at least, which had been unable or unwilling to be part of the regime. We accepted as natural the idea of hiding our true circumstances, and if someone had told us that in doing so we were conforming to the prejudices, the inability to confront reality, and the fundamental apathy of the classes we came from, and not, instead, the laws of dignity and decorum, we would have rebelled. Myself above all. Let me add, further, that we were originally from the south, and had come with traditions and customs as firm as irrevocable principles, and so it was difficult to assimilate or be assimilated into Genoese society. And the particular disfiguring atmosphere of Fascist reality also weighed heavily on us. The official optimism of the regime did not admit or tolerate economic catastrophe. We who were not infected by Fascism saw clearly the unbridgeable gap between reality and the official optimism, but I think that this, in the end, even if we were unconscious of it, in some way legitimized what we considered dignity and decorum. All these elements were at the source of that phase of our family's isolation that ended when, a few years later, Paolo, Maria Luisa, and, finally, I began working, and the situation partly improved. But starting in 1938, unfortunately, our isolation was enforced by law.

After 1935, as I said, the Jewish exiles from Hitler's Germany ceased to knock at our door. But, that same year, Fascism set off on its own brutal adventures and Nazism stood at its side. Later, there were days when our emaciated and terrorized visitors of earlier times seemed to peep out from the big war headlines in the newspapers, and we felt their vague and shadowy presence near us as indistinct fears that we did not speak of with each other.

Our family, meanwhile, was regaining a certain economic ease. Paolo got a job at the Venice General Insurance Company, Roberto at the National Institute of Insurance, and Maria Luisa at the state banana monopoly. Giorgio was studying at the Tortelli Technical Institute and Bice and I at the Regina Elena Business College.

The racial laws went into effect unexpectedly in August 1938. Some time earlier, the Fascist government had declared that in Italy the "Jewish question" did not exist. And so the event took us by surprise: a lightning bolt striking our house. In the course of a few days Paolo, Roberto, and Maria Luisa lost their jobs. In October Giorgio, Bice, and I had to leave the state schools and enroll in the Jewish school. I was then sixteen years old, an age when young people, in general, have a lively critical sense and, with it, begin to confront and judge life. My sisters and I had been reared and educated according to principles that prevented us from having any contact with people of our own age, with society, with the world. We were kept in the dark about all aspects of family affairs that pertained exclusively to our parents, and in general they avoided discussing in front of us any subject apart from simple domestic relations. It may seem absurd, but I don't know what my brothers were earning at the time. And it would have been vain to seek the cause of our own difficulties or of those which occurred outside the magic circle of our family.

We were a family of lambs, good people, ready to suffer any wrongs rather than be stained by a single one, eager to make as little noise as possible and occupy the least space possible on this earth. Even the night when Paolo, Roberto, and Maria Luisa announced that they had lost their jobs and the vortex of the future opened before us, we did not complain, remaining silent so that no one would hear us, meditating on the terrible unknown of the next day. In my mind the memories of the events of those days are confused.

Papa was pessimistic, and he realized that, at least in official relations with firms, his profession, if he had never had much success, would from now on be absolutely fruitless. Mamma, who perhaps better than all of us sensed the dimensions of our present and of our brief future, aged rapidly in a few days, enveloped in an increasingly desperate silence. Roberto and Maria Luisa seemed the most optimistic and with their words they encouraged the rest of us. But beneath the more immediate worries, in the depths of our anxieties, was the sensation that something calamitous was about to overwhelm us. Yet again we discovered that our visitors of 1934 and 1935 had left in our house and in us a thick, almost concrete presence that was beginning to have a shape. The Germany of Hitler, which had seemed so far away, was becoming confused with our own land, the land of our birth, my land and that of my fore-bears. The reality that we had wanted to ignore suddenly, and in its most brutal form, possessed us.

The first discriminations and the first bans were followed by others. No day passed that August and in the following months when the papers did not carry the text of some new sanction against the Jews. Progressively, day by day, our margin of liberty and life was reduced.

Reports began to circulate regarding Jewish families who were leaving Italy. Many of them emigrated to France, in the illusion that they would be safe there. A year later, all of Europe had become a tomb for Jews wherever they were. The fortunate were those who managed to reach the two Americas.

In that summer of 1938, the orders leading to our declassification to the rank of subhumans were published, and the racial campaign gained noticeable strength—in particular in the press, with articles and essays to which men who called themselves scientists lent themselves. There were others, too, whose names I see sometimes even today among the defenders of "civilization," the same "civilization" as then, which has merely changed its label. We often left our house looking at the people we were used to, and to whom we belonged, in fear and distrust: as if we were afraid that the anti-Semitic campaign could incite even ordinary men against us. Indeed, at first my brothers were worried that something like that might happen. And yet not only then but, above all, in the years that followed, we discovered around us a silent yet active human solidarity. The anti-Jewish measures generally aroused new impulses against the Fascist dictatorship and more sympathy toward us than we had ever felt before. Proof of this lies in the fact that in the autumn following that summer of anguish, Paolo was hired by the firm Fratelli Schiavetti, Roberto by Terracini, and Maria Luisa first by the office of the lawyer Greco and later by that of the lawyers Sciarretta and Medina. In 1941 I got a job at the S.A.I.C., owned by Morelli and Ginepro, replacing a German Jew who had been imprisoned in a concentration camp in Montefiascone. All of us in applying for jobs had to declare that we were Jewish, but this—except in some cases of "prudence"—only provoked open anti-Fascist declarations, often made in a tone of relief, as if the speaker had at last found someone he could be sure of trusting.

If the trial of the Italian Jews, even after September 8, 1943, did not attain the tragic proportions suffered by Jews elsewhere, that was due to the marvelous and human conscience of our people. And I believe that my testimony may be more valuable because during the year that we lived in hiding, assailed and tormented by the nightmare, closer and closer to our horrendous end, I was able to experience and appreciate the truth of what I am saying. I recall a poor peasant of Sampierdicanne, near Chiavari, where we had been evacuated, repeating that humanity is divided not between Jews and non-Jews but between rich and poor, between those who possess everything and those who possess nothing, between those who work the land and do not enjoy its fruits and those who do not work the land and appropriate for themselves the harvest of field and vineyard. These words of ancient wisdom have remained in my heart, and I am certain that they contain a profound popular truth. I, an Italian Jew, felt their value at a time when my mere existence represented a crime punishable by death.

On September 8, for the first time, Paolo was asked to go to Novi Ligure by the directors of the firm he worked for. Having finished his assignment, he came to see me, and when he entered my office I was so unprepared to see him that I barely recognized him. At the end of the day, I introduced him to my colleague and we went out. I was really pleased by this unexpected meeting and only worried that Paolo would ask to see my living arrangements in Novi Ligure, where the S.A.I.C. had moved its offices because of the constant bombardments in Genoa. I had had to insist with my father to let me go with Morelli and Ginepro. Some time earlier my family had been evacuated to Sampierdicanne, a few kilometers from Chiavari, and so I had to spend the whole week away from them. I left from Chiavari on Monday at dawn and returned the following Saturday evening. In the hours that I spent with the family Papa did his best to convince me that I should give up the job and stay home. It seemed extraordinary to him that two of his daughters worked, but it was utterly inconceivable that one of them was away from home for six days out of the seven. Papa had had to give up every activity himself, and he would endure any sacrifice in order not to make the family situation worse. He was no longer the man I recalled from the past: his features were unchanged, but he had aged beyond his years. To us it seemed that our mother now had seven children rather than six, and one of them was our father. I would have been happy not to work and live alone in Novi Ligure, but I couldn't let my family go without my salary, for we were already in serious difficulties. Besides, my mother's attitude, when Papa persisted in his arguments, was sufficient to make me understand how necessary it was that I continue to work. Bit by bit I managed to calm Papa, by leading him to believe that I was decently settled in Novi and had everything I needed. In truth the whole clerical staff employed by the S.A.I.C. in Novi consisted of my colleague, Signor Mantelli, and me. Signor Mantelli had moved with his family and so he, of course, needed a large room. I had ended up in a room carved out of the attic, a tiny room with a low, sloping ceiling that followed the incline of the roof. I didn't complain because, at heart, I enjoyed an independence I had never had before and, once the shock of adapting was over, I liked even the strange position of the bed, from which I could see the progressive descent of the ceiling. No one, not even Paolo, would have been able to appreciate what I called my comforts. For this reason I was afraid that, if he laid eyes on the attic, my brother would return home scandalized, and that would provoke my immediate recall. I remember all this because it was what was worrying me in the last hours of September 8, 1943.

I managed to keep Paolo from getting interested in my lodgings and we went to dine in a small trattoria. We had just begun to eat when over the radio came the announcement of the armistice. It was still daylight and people were coming and going on the streets of Novi. Suddenly, it was as if the city and its inhabitants had been stricken by paralysis: silence fell while the announcer proceeded to read the communiqué. I was attentive, but I understood only that the war was over, and already I was thinking that the next day we would no longer have to fear the sky; the bombs would stop and, with that, the nightmare would dissolve. I couldn't understand Paolo's attitude as he sat opposite me, his face becoming more and more tense and preoccupied. When the announcer was silent, a tumult of cries arose in the restaurant and on the streets. Paolo pushed back his plate and stood up.

"Come with me immediately," he said. "We have to go home right away."

I asked him why.

"There is trouble ahead," he answered.

"The war is over . . ." I repeated.

"Not for the Germans," my brother said.

I had the impression that he knew something that he did not intend to share with me. Inside I felt the desire to sing and shout as I saw other people doing on the streets. Paolo asked me where we would find my bosses at that hour. We went to the office, where we found only Signor Morelli, intent on his work. He, too, had heard on the radio the news of the armistice. In a few days the Allies would occupy Italy and expel the Germans, he said. My brother told him he had decided to take me home. Morelli commented on Paolo's reaction, calling it exaggerated.

"Whatever may happen, Signorina Sonnino runs no risk as long as she remains with us."

My brother insisted. He repeated that for the Germans the war wasn't over, and it meant one didn't know them if one believed that they would so easily abandon Italy. Morelli argued that there were enough of our soldiers in Italy to confront any threat from the Germans. Paolo wished him well and hoped that things would go according to his predictions.

We took leave of my boss, whom I never saw again after that day. I gathered up my few things and we set off for Sampierdicanne. During the train journey fragments of conversations overheard among the passengers, the atmosphere of the car, the confusion

I noticed in the stations, and the appearance of German uniforms in places where I had never seen them began to convince me that my brother's presentiments of danger were not in fact exaggerated.

When we arrived at Sampierdicanne we found our family in a state of alarm. From Chiavari and from Genoa news continued to arrive about threatening movements of German troops and the early breakup of the Italian divisions. Before reaching home we had met numerous soldiers asking for civilian clothes. One of them said that the other officers had vanished. In the middle of the night the rumor spread that the barracks in Genoa were already under German control and that the Italian soldiers who hadn't escaped had been made prisoners. It was impossible to find confirmation of so many reports and rumors, in part, too, because they contradicted one another. People said that Alpine divisions were approaching, and waited to be liberated by them. Already on that night, however, the general sense was of a nearly total dissolution of the standards and rules that until then had helped us to live and on which we had modeled ourselves.

My father and my brothers talked until dawn and decided that we had better leave Sampierdicanne immediately and find a secure hiding place. I have the impression, as I write these lines, that that night, perhaps unconsciously, we reached the conclusion of a process that had long been maturing within us. Without being aware of it, we had always known, after 1938 and perhaps even before—perhaps ever since Nazi anti-Semitism had sent us its first witnesses—that the moment would come when we would have to flee, and we were prepared for it, as an ineluctable fate.

The next day the catastrophe was revealed in all its dimensions. The Nazi troops by now were in control of the situation. In the stations and along the streets they pursued the Italian soldiers. Chiavari, in a few hours, had changed its aspect. Maria Luisa returned that evening from Genoa with even more calamitous news.

Our city had been invaded and there was tremendous anguish everywhere.

The situation seemed desperate. Although Paolo and Roberto, as Jews, had been exempted from

49

military service, they could be captured by the Germans as deserting soldiers, and in that case they could expect much worse than prison. We would need false identity cards, but neither our father nor my brothers knew how to obtain them. Suddenly we found ourselves like a hare flushed out of the woods by a pack of dogs and caught in the open, with no defense. The time of illusions had gone forever, and now, with the Germans masters of our land and of our fate, we knew, at least in part, what awaited us.

For the moment we decided that the boys should remain hidden at home while we women would do all we could to find a way to safety. Twice in the following days we experienced concretely the human solidarity that up until then had supported us; twice solutions were offered that could have saved our lives.

Maria Luisa continued to come and go from Genoa; she was the only one who had kept her job. At the end of September it appeared urgent that we leave Sampierdicanne, because the area by now had become particularly dangerous for our brothers. Maria Luisa was therefore advised to quit her job. The lawyer Sciarretta understood our troubles completely and told my sister that if we would like he could find a safe refuge for us. We were to go to Termini* and there talk to his brother, who would provide for us. He was aware of our difficult economic situation, and was also willing to make available to us the means for the journey.

When Maria Luisa came home and told us about this proposal, we all drew a sigh of relief. A glimmer of light appeared before us, that, however faint, represented something less uncertain than the conditions in which we were living. Enthusiastically we began to discuss the journey and what we would find in Termini. Mamma listened, and then pointed out to us, in her always calm voice, that for our

---

* This is the only passage that is not clear. Piera Sonnino's daughter Bice vaguely recalls her mother telling of a job in Terni to which Ettore Sonnino was opposed. Terni was liberated by the Allies in June 1943. So it can't be the place that Piera is referring to, which was liberated, rather, between the end of September and the beginning of October. It's more likely that the text alludes to Termoli, in the province of Campobasso (at the time in the region of Abruzzo-Molise), which was taken by Montgomery's VIII Army on October 3, 1943. Bearing out this hypothesis is the fact that the surname Sciarretta is common in the area, and in the text it is said

brothers it would be a huge risk. Paolo, Roberto, and Giorgio faced the danger of being captured by the Germans as soon as they set foot outside the house.

Paolo and Roberto admitted that what Mamma said was true and proposed that we should split up. Our parents and we three sisters would leave for Termini, and Paolo, Roberto, and Giorgio would try to get to Switzerland. The boys, like the rest of us, were aware that, the day after September 8, an organization had appeared, as if out of nowhere—or perhaps it had already been active in occupied Italy—that was particularly effective in getting Jews to Swiss territory. The

that the lawyer's brother lived there. With the failure of the "Termini" prospect, the lawyer proposes a "monastery in the Abruzzo." One can also exclude the possibility that the reference is to the village of Termine, also in Abruzzo, near Mt. Terminillo. The reasons are three: that area was liberated some months later; the town is so small that Sonnino, usually so precise, would surely have felt the need to provide some further information; and it is unlikely that the news of its liberation could have arrived in only a day, as it says further on in the text. Finally, the hypothesis of Termine di Roverano on Mt. Bracco, in Liguria, is improbable, because a destination so close would not have posed so many uncertainties for the Sonnino family.

center of the organization was in Milan. Naturally it would take money to cross the border and more money was needed to live in Switzerland. We had none and, knowing that, hadn't even considered that avenue of escape. But, even more than the lack of money, the influence of the magic family circle, and the place we were used to, continued to act on us. Going to Switzerland bore the aspect of an adventure beyond the possible, an inconceivable uprooting. I think that this is the truth because for a year we traveled in circles, remaining essentially at the same point, as we waited for our destiny to fulfill itself. Today it may appear absurd, certainly childish, but that is what happened.

Paolo and Roberto were sure that in Switzerland they would manage even without money. Together with Giorgio, Roberto said, they were six arms at the disposal of three stomachs.

Mother and father definitively opposed this solution. Mamma claimed that the risk our brothers would run in getting to Switzerland was no smaller than that presented by the journey from Genoa to Termini. Maybe it was larger. She said that she would never forgive herself for being in a safe place while her three sons were left to the mercy of chance. She began to cry as if she already imagined herself far away from the boys, tormenting herself about their fate. Papa, for his part, declared that if there was danger we must confront it together. Everywhere. Paolo and Roberto were insistent. For several years a sister of Mamma's, Aunt Anna Milani, had been living with us; we were a family of nine people, an army, as Roberto put it. To try to travel all together, he asserted, was madness. It was a second exodus that would not go unobserved. We five women, led by Papa, would have every possibility of arriving safely at Termini, and there could wait for the end of the war. We continued to discuss and discuss, and finally Mamma won the day: we would all attempt the journey to Termini together.

Maria Luisa returned to Sciarretta to tell him our decision. The lawyer interrupted her halfway through her speech: Termini had been occupied by Allied troops the day before. He spread his arms and said he had offered us that possibility at the right moment. Again we fell into despair.

Sampierdicanne and the whole area of Chiavari were permanently patrolled by Nazi and Fascist troops. Our brothers were living in imminent and continuous danger. Maria Luisa went back to Sciarretta. He was understanding and suggested a monastery in the Abruzzo whose prior he knew. Yet again he offered us money. And again we began our discussion, this time, based on our earlier experience, keeping in mind the possibility that the part of the Abruzzo he had mentioned might be occupied before we got there. In that case—if the occupation should occur while we were en route—what would we do? We ended up by rejecting definitively this second chance for safety.

At the end of September and the beginning of October, it was clear that if we delayed our departure from Sampierdicanne by even a single day we would run the risk of being caught by the Germans. More than one person in that area was aware that we were Jews. Roberto decided to ask for help from a colleague in his office, Signora Maria Luisa Bancalari. Overcoming Mamma's reluctance, and her anxiety about his going to Genoa, he went to see Signora Bancalari and returned saying that, through her maid, she could find us a place in Val Trebbia—more precisely, in a village near Rovegno. We waited anxiously for a few days, and finally Signora Bancalari told us that there were some rooms available in the only inn in Pietranera di Rovegno, which had been closed for months, and that a peasant was willing to provide us with a kitchen. One morning we piled our things on a cart and on foot left Chiavari. Around us quite a few people gathered, both curious and compassionate, to see "the Jewish family" leaving. They looked at us with something in their eyes that I will never forget. If my brothers had asked, I am certain that they would have helped us put our bags on the cart and would have shaken hands with us all if we had held them out first. As we set off we couldn't help thinking of those people and of the fact that, although each of us was worth a reward of two thousand *lire*, no one had reported us. We were leaving behind us poor, humble, unknown people, people who possessed absolutely nothing and who had given us a few months more of life.

The journey to Pietranera di Rovegno was frightening, filled with moments of alarm. There were German and republican soldiers everywhere: this meant hours of agony for us, and even more for our brothers, who could be captured at any moment.

Autumn had already come to Pietranera. The leaves on the trees were yellow and the meadows showed rich traces of green mixed with gray and brown patches. The valley of the Trebbia was swept by the first cold winds. The inn was even more modest than we had imagined. It seemed to have been abandoned and deserted for centuries. We settled as best we could in the rooms indicated to us. We began an existence that was completely different from anything we were used to. We had absolutely nothing to do. As long as we could, we spent the days walking in the woods, always vigilant, and careful not to call attention to ourselves. In the evening we went to bed early, and I remember my long, heavy dreamless sleeps. We girls prepared meals in the kitchen, which was a hundred meters from the inn. They were meals that did not require much work: polenta, dried chestnuts, chestnuts newly fallen from the trees, chestnut flour. Potatoes were a luxury, and we owed it to Roberto, who went around to the neighboring farms and villages, if we ate them from time to time. Signora Bancalari more than once sent us packages containing pasta and other provisions, and those days were a celebration for us.

The tension did not diminish. We were in a continuous state of anxiety. The area was traversed almost daily by German divisions headed for the mountains. Whenever they appeared we abandoned the inn or the kitchen and scattered in the woods. One day we fled at the approach of men in uniform and on our return learned that they were English soldiers who had escaped from a prison camp. No one told us why they had passed through Pietranera. For more than a month we lived at the edge of an area controlled largely by the partisans and we didn't know it. We had safety within reach and didn't realize it. Only when I came back from the camps did I learn what the mountains that surrounded us concealed. And I also learned what bonds there were between those mountains and the peasants who protected us, too, with their silence.

Winter arrived, and it was frigid. We couldn't light a fire in the inn, so we became used to living in the kitchen, where a big, red-hot stove roared without interruption. We considered ourselves very fortunate for the way things had turned out.

An invitation from the marshal at the *carabinieri* headquarters at Rovegno caught us unawares. He asked if one of us could come and talk with him. At first we were terrified, but Roberto pointed out that if it had been what we feared they would have come and captured us without an invitation and without warning. He said that probably it was a request for information, since we had been at Pietranera for some time and hadn't reported our presence. We decided that Roberto should meet with the marshal of the *carabinieri*. He left early one morning when it was snowing, and he returned around midday. Every trace of optimism had disappeared from his face. We gathered around him in the kitchen and he told us how things had gone. The marshal had been very kind. "In asking you to come here," he had said, "I expose myself and my men to a risk that you can very easily assess. We have known for some time that your family is Jewish. Unfortunately, we are not the only ones who know it. The news has traveled. If someone should inform the Germans, we, too, would suffer the consequences for not having reported you in a timely manner. Certainly we will not be the ones who hand you over to the German command. However, in both your interest and ours, you must leave Pietranera immediately. All I can do for you is advise you to go."

Roberto had asked for a few days to look for some other town where we might find refuge, and the marshal, in the end, had granted that. Roberto had lunch and left immediately to search for a new hiding place. He said that he would introduce himself as an evacuee from Genoa looking for lodgings for his family. The first peasant he asked told him that he wouldn't know where to shelter him. Suddenly he lowered his voice and confided to Roberto that the area was dangerous for everyone. Roberto asked him why and the peasant looked at him a long time before answering. Finally he told him that a family of Jews was hiding in the neighborhood and that one day or another the Germans would surely find out and then it would be trouble for everyone. For the Jews, he said, and for us who have been silent about it. Roberto hurried away. He wandered in vain all afternoon. The peasants had no room for evacuees. They were vague, circumspect, distrustful. More than once their words betrayed a sense of the dangerousness of that countryside, because the mountains were so close, and for other reasons as well. He heard the Jewish family mentioned other times, too.

In the following days Roberto continued to look for somewhere for us to hide, and finally he had to give up. There was no place for strangers in those hills and mountains. In his days of anguished searching he had come to see the truth of what the marshal of Rovegno said, and another fact, much more important: as in Sampierdicanne, here in Pietranera we had been protected and saved by the people's silence.

When the deadline we had been given arrived, we had to prepare to leave.

We left Pietranera in the depths of night, dividing into two groups, slipping and sliding along the wet paths among trees that were now, in winter, bare. The cold was intense. The sky was frozen, like the moon that illuminated the way.

A bus brought us to Prato, on the far outskirts of Genoa. We preferred to get off there rather than go into the center, not knowing what we would find. We had returned to the point of departure. We found ourselves, with the few things we had brought from Pietranera, in an unknown place, on the threshold of a city that no longer ours, that appeared to us an enormous trap to which, ineluctably, we were condemned to return. Our flight, and still we did not know it, was over. Now, leaning against the little wall overlooking the Bisagno,* we didn't know where to go or what to do. It was as if we had been shipwrecked in an unknown land. The difference was that the danger was immediate. People looked at us with curiosity. There were many soldiers around: it would have been enough for one of them to ask us for our identity cards. I can't remember how long we remained there debating, more within ourselves than among ourselves, that terrible and paradoxical situation. Maria Luisa finally decided to telephone Perla Moroni, a colleague in the office of Sciarretta and Medina. We looked for a bar with a telephone and waited for our sister. We didn't hide from ourselves the precariousness of the attempt: Maria Luisa's friend might not be in the office that day, or might not want to get involved in our problem because of the danger it entailed. It was also possible that in spite of her good will she wouldn't know where to direct us or how to help us.

* The river that crosses the city of Genoa.

Waiting for Maria Luisa to return was nerve-racking. We were afraid even to look at one another. Finally our sister came out of the bar. She waved a hand in our direction: Perla Moroni was waiting for her in the office. She would give us the keys to a vacant apartment in a damaged building on Via Archimede.

We stayed in that apartment for a month. The windows had no glass and there was no heat. We had neither light nor gas, but the house felt like a palace. We were safe there. All nine of us had to settle ourselves in a single room because the others were full of furniture, but having to spend hours without moving, in order not to bump against one another, did not seem too great a sacrifice.

After a month we had to leave: Signorina Moroni let us know that the house was no longer safe.

Once again we found ourselves caught up in the drastic problem of looking for a place to hide. Signora Bancalara, who had already helped us by finding the hotel in Pietranera, managed to find an apartment for us in Carignano. Like the one on Via Archimede, the new house was damaged. The day we arrived we realized that it was a provisional stop and that we would have to find something less risky. Roberto again took charge. A priest[*] whom he knew through a friend rented, in his own name, an apartment on Via Montallegro, and after a month in Carignano we went to live there. The priest, also in his own name, made sure that the apartment had electricity and gas.

My family had lived in Via Montallegro when we moved from Milan to Genoa. Our story, which had practically begun on that street, would end on the same pavement, within the same walls, in the same setting.

I have very vivid memories of the period of nine months that we spent on Via Montallegro: memories bound together by the anguish that filled our days. They were nine months of the most acute tension, without an instant of relief. Paolo and Roberto had of necessity to obtain the means for us to live. In their situation it was anything but easy to look for work. From the moment they left in the morning

---

[*] Speaking to Chiara Borelli on February 23, 1998, under the auspices of Steven Spielberg's project *Survivors of the Shoah*, Sonnino gives this priest a name: Don Repetto. This was Don Francesco Repetto, who was secretary to the cardinal of Genoa, Pietro Boetto, and among the Righteous of Italy.

until their return, we lived in fear of their capture. Paolo managed to find bookkeeping jobs in small businesses and some students for private lessons. Among these was a *carabiniere* who got so involved in our situation that he had false ration cards made for us. Roberto, thanks to contacts he had made when he worked at the fabric company Terracini, was able to get work in the same business. I see him again, leaving the house with his sample case under his arm. Papa had collapsed. He walked with a cane. He was a man reduced, overwhelmed by a cataclysm that annihilated him because he had nothing to fight it with, no strength at all.

Giorgio's situation was undoubtedly the most dire. Giorgio had grown up first in the world of discrimination, and then in that of the nightmare. He didn't know the meaning of childhood and adolescence; he had remained an infant, attached to our mother by a bond that grew increasingly morbid. He was a gentle soul. When he suffered panic attacks—and this happened often—we were thrown into dismay. His quick and lively intelligence was undoubtedly the cause of his torment, of the depth of the tragedy he endured, of the abnormal sensitivity he developed, intensifying all his feelings.

In those nine months, two things happened, of scant importance in themselves but for us notable. On August 16, 1944, as I was making some purchases at the market of Via XX Settembre, I felt a tug on the purse that I carried over my arm, and the individual who had grabbed it fled. Some men who were there chased him and managed to catch him. The purse was restored to me and I was asked if I wanted to file a report against the thief.* I had already answered no when a policeman in civilian clothes intervened. He was an extraordinarily ceremonious man who insisted that it was my duty as a citizen to punish the thief. I was rigid with fear. I tried to resist the policeman and, seeing my efforts were useless, burst into tears. I wept desperately because I realized the danger I would be in if I went

* Also in the interview for *Survivors of the Shoah*, Sonnino says: "The thief was a man who had just been released from the Savona prison. . . . I've always been unable to bear this business of being robbed, which might have attracted attention, which might have been my fault. . . . Crazy."

to a police station. I looked for a way out, but it was impossible: the policeman, the thief, and I were surrounded by a knot of curious bystanders. The three of us set off for the police station that was then situated on the first floor of the Palazzo Ducale. The policeman couldn't understand why I was crying and attributed it to the shock.

In front of the official, as I was giving my information, I was assailed by another wave of panic. On Via Montallegro we called ourselves Melani, but a childish trick with the police would be useless. The official asked for my identity card. I was trembling when I took it out. Fortunately it still bore the address on Via Montello that we had left when we were evacuated to Chiavari and where we had not returned. Coldly the official recorded name, surname, and address and asked me to sign the report. I did so, and I don't know how I managed to control my hand for that instant. I asked if I could go and was told yes. I left the police station in a hurry, with my heart in my throat. I ran into Paolo in Piazza De Ferrari and told him the story. My brother reproached me firmly for my inattention. I pointed out that it wasn't my fault, and he said that it was: if I had been more attentive, the thief would not have snatched my purse. The next day the news was in the papers. Fifteen lines that reported everything about me. For a long time I was gnawed by the suspicion that it was that news item that had put the Germans on our trail. It was an absurd suspicion, but it was a long time before I could free myself from it.

Papa was the protagonist of the second incident. At the end of September he was the victim of an accident that could have accelerated the moment of our capture. That day he had gone out for a short walk when he fell and fractured his shoulder. He had to defend himself not so much from the pain as from those who wanted to help him by taking him to the hospital of San Martino, just a few hundred meters from where he had fallen. Finally he was brought home. We turned to Professor Pasquale Cattaneo, whom we knew we could trust, and he promised that he would send a colleague. Papa's shoulder was put in a cast, and the cast was still there on the morning of October 12 and during the night of the twenty-seventh and the twenty-eighth, the long, tortured night of Auschwitz.

October 12, 1944, was a day that began under an intensely blue sky, crystal clear, with summer fading and the first cool autumn breezes. Torrents of light from the garden inundated our house on Via Montallegro. I remember every moment of that day, every image. I see my mother and father in their big double bed, aged by now and worn out with suffering, turn their heads toward me as I come in to say good morning, and I feel, I feel their eyes on my face as if they were flames. A morning like any other: like millions of others that preceded it and would follow. But for us unique, different from any other morning, of the past or of the future. It contains the last images of what until then we were, images of my family, of my parents, of my brothers and sisters. Everything that happened in those hours was happening for the last time. And there was no forewarning. We lived those hours as usual, prisoners of the usual fear, of anxiety. My father and mother in the double bed: this is the last memory I have preserved of them, still creatures of this earth, still woman and man, still human.

I went out at around eight-thirty to the market on Via Dante. It was just after ten when I got on the tram to go home. Along the way I noted on the street the scenes of every day: the sight of every German and Fascist uniform alarmed me, and whenever the tram slowed down for any reason I trembled, afraid of a sudden round-up. It was now late morning, and the soldiers at times appeared to me as what they were: men. Sometimes, when fear broke the thin barrier erected by reason, they were like black stains, the black outlines of the nightmare in which we were struggling.

When we passed the Casa dello Studente,[*]
I stepped onto the rear platform of the tram, preparing to get off. At the Via Papigliano stop, the next to last before Piazza San Martino, Bice was waiting for me. I saw her as the tram was about to stop, leaning forward to look for me. She beckoned me toward her. She was very pale. Her eyes were red. I recall every word of our brief, agitated dialogue.

"I've been waiting more than half an hour for you. They came to take Papa."

"When and who came to take our father?"

"Two officers in civilian clothes. Papa had just got up. They know who we are."

"Where did they take him?"

"To the Casa dello Studente, they said. They took Papa . . . they took Papa. . . ." Bice kept repeating. The bag I had hanging on my arm suddenly seemed incredibly heavy. I couldn't think. My mind was blank. I took Bice by the hand. My sister was burning as if she had a fever. She said that Mamma had already telephoned Paolo and Roberto to come

---

[*] The Nazi-Fascist headquarters was situated there.

home right away. We were to meet at Piazza San Martino and flee immediately, together. Soon they will come and take us, we have to hurry. We walked quickly, as if hallucinating; to me it seemed we were moving in the darkness of a tunnel, I saw nothing around me, neither the houses nor the passersby. Bice was a few steps ahead of me when, from Via Papigliano, we reached Piazza San Martino. Our mother, our brothers, and Maria Luisa should have been at the tram stop. Bice turned toward me disconsolate. Not a single member of our family was at the meeting place we had agreed on.

As we turned onto Via Montallegro, we still had an absurd hope that Mamma and the boys had, for some reason or other, been forced not to wait for us but had already reached safety. Bice and I would somehow manage to track them down and join them. The important thing was that they had left the house. The hope lasted a few seconds. In front of the garden gate of our house two men were stationed. We could immediately guess who they were. The worst had happened. We stopped for a moment. The two had seen us, but paid scant attention. We still had time to turn and flee. We would have only to go back the way we came as if it were natural. Aunt Anna was away from home, we could wait for her and then the three of us could again confront our fate. Try to save ourselves, to survive. I think that neither in Bice nor in me, not even for an instant, did such thoughts arise. We started walking again, holding each other by the hand, knowing perfectly well where we were going. Where we had to go. Our mother, Paolo, Roberto, Giorgio, and Maria Luisa were inside, as if they were waiting for us. And they were waiting for us.

One of the two agents came over and spoke to me.

"Are you Signorina Melani? . . . Excuse me, Signorina Sonnino?"

I said yes.

"And this is your sister, right?" He was almost kind.

"Please, ladies, make yourselves comfortable over here."

We crossed the garden and went up the stairs that led to our parents' bedroom. Mamma and the boys were there. An incredible confusion reigned in the room. Mamma had thrown herself onto the bed, weeping. She was wearing her usual black dress: she had been ready to leave when the police arrived. Maria Luisa was beside her. Her arms were around Mamma's shoulders. Paolo and Roberto were talking to two other agents. The arrest occurred in a way that none of us had foreseen. Even the police seemed different from how we had imagined them. They observed us with a kind of indifference, but they were not impatient.

Roberto was saying to them: "Take us men and let the women stay. My mother is old. Look at her," he told the policeman. "Where would you take her, to jail?"

The policeman shrugged his shoulders. They had orders to arrest all the members of the family. A family of Jews, he said emphatically, with a faint sneer. And he immediately went on to say that he didn't understand all the commotion. He spoke with a southern accent that distorted his words. Another policeman interrupted him and joined in as if he were speaking to himself: "Jews . . . really Jews. They crucified our Lord Jesus Christ, the Jews." He turned to us, also with a faint sneer. "What trouble you've been in since then. What a lot of trouble. And who could pay attention to you after what you did?" The first starts saying again that there's no point weeping and crying. He has orders to accompany us to the Casa dello Studente: there we will be asked to sign a document in which we pledge to work for Germany, after which the business will be finished and we can return home.

Roberto controlled himself with difficulty. Paolo stopped arguing. Giorgio had crumpled onto a chair. He seemed without life. In the intervals of silence our sobs could be heard. The police ordered us to get ready. We had to go. Roberto and Paolo made the last, useless attempts to persuade them to leave Mamma and us sisters. We talked and cried, weeping together. The policemen looked out the door, across the garden, and onto the street, as if to check if anyone could hear us. "Let's not make all that noise!" they said. "Let's not make all that noise!"

"Signora," one of them said to Mamma, "it's just a short walk. From here to the Casa dello Studente. How far? Two hundred meters. In an hour you'll be back home with your children and your husband."

Those words, those minutes, seem unreal, fantastic now in memory. And yet they are words heard and minutes lived just as I am recounting them. We had imagined our arrest as a cyclone that would suddenly sweep down upon us, and instead it came almost silently, swaddled in that evil and pointless lie.

Finally we became decisive. Maria Luisa and Bice were allowed to go to their room to get some clothes. Roberto said that we had a small sum of money in the house and asked if he could entrust it to our neighbor, Alessandro Trolli, an old and distinguished gentleman who lived in the apartment above ours, with his sick wife and a daughter. Signor Trolli, as I later heard from Roberto, was very kind. Roberto explained who we were and why they were arresting us, and Signor Trolli, despite the presence of the policeman who accompanied my brother, said it was a crime to persecute innocent people. He also said that he deeply regretted what was occurring and would be happy to be of help. He declared that he was willing to keep whatever amount we considered it prudent to entrust to him, and that we could be sure of finding it untouched upon our return.

Only when I returned did I understand the generosity shown by the police in allowing us to entrust the money to Signor Trolli, and I can never forget that man's honest resolve.

As soon as we were led away, in fact, two officers returned to our neighbor to ask that he immediately hand over the money that we had entrusted to him. Signor Trolli refused their request and resisted their threats. In the following days they tried again to get our money from him, but in vain. When I returned, I found the sum deposited in a bank under my family's name.

We left our house single file. The police had ordered us not to call attention to ourselves. Along the way they said to Maria Luisa, who was still crying, "Come, signorina, stop it. Please. Tell us what we've done to you or what we've said to make you cry like that!"

I don't know what happened to those police-men, if they are dead or if they are alive, I don't know what job they have now or what profession they practice; but perhaps their children are grown men, as Paolo and Roberto were then, or young women like Maria Luisa and me, or children like Giorgio and Bice.

The person who ordered our arrest was Brenno Grandi, who was acquitted, in a trial in 1947, because he managed to show that he had not been cruel to Jews for his personal gain; but those four agents who carried out his orders, wherever they might be today, I want them to know that the moment they dragged us from our house, that first and only time they saw us, they started us on our journey toward death. For me today, in my memory, they have the face of death.

Halfway along Via Papigliano we saw Aunt Anna, who, panting, was returning home. Aunt Anna saw us and stopped suddenly. Roberto made a gesture to her with his hand that the police, although they were watching us carefully, didn't see or didn't understand. Aunt Anna, however, understood perfectly, and we saw her disappear into a shop. She was the only one of us who was not deported.

Suddenly, a little farther on, Roberto became animated and called to someone who was walking on the opposite sidewalk. A friend, he said in a low voice, indicating a man who was crossing the street to join us. A big shot at the Casa dello Studente. Maybe he'll help us.

He was a young man, barely over twenty. He listened to Roberto in silence and looked us in the face one by one. He joined us and entered the Casa dello Studente with us. Casually he proceeded to an office with a big sign in German over the door. He knocked and, on being told to come in, made a sign to us to enter. The office was quite large. Behind a desk sat a German officer.

"Hello!" said Roberto's friend. "Good catch this morning. An entire Jewish family. Congratulations." He exchanged a greeting with the officer, who shook his hand, and he left without a glance at us.

They recorded our names carefully and made us sign a paper. Some guards then led us down to the basement and opened the door of a cell. Mamma entered first and cried, "Ettore . . ."

Our father was sitting on a bench fixed to the wall, weeping desperately. We didn't even hear the door of the cell close behind us. Papa told us between sobs that they had interrogated him at length, asking where Paolo, Roberto, and Giorgio were, and he had said that he didn't know.

"Did they beat you?" Mamma asked.

Papa shook his head no.

The cell was tiny. The eight of us crowded it. We had to take turns sitting on the bench or the ground. We cried for a long time, holding one another, we sisters and our mother, with Giorgio, who was overcome by fear, in the middle. Roberto at a certain point began pounding on the door with his fists. A peephole opened and two eyes examined him.

"Bring something for these women to eat!" my brother cried. The peephole was closed. After a quarter of an hour some food was brought, which none of us touched. Roberto himself tried to eat but spit out the only bit he managed to get in his mouth. Paolo kept wondering who had betrayed and reported us.* He ended up getting Roberto involved, too. They reviewed all the people they knew and dismissed each one. Roberto said that the circumstances of our

---

* After she returned, Sonnino was sure that the person who had told the police about the family's presence was a Signora Grossi, who lived in the same apartment building on Via Montallegro. The nephew of this woman became a schoolmate of her older daughter, Bice. It was Colonel Brenno Grandi who ordered the arrest, and, according to Sonnino, collected fifty thousand *lire* for the capture of eight Jews. Nevertheless, after the war Brenno Grandi was acquitted of the charge that he had acted for personal gain.

arrest proved that the Nazis and Fascists of the anti-Jewish section of the Casa dello Studente had only scant and vague information about us. If they had been absolutely certain that we were Jews they would have arrested us all sometime during the night, or at midday or in the evening.

A few hours after sunset we were taken out of the cell, loaded into a prison truck, and transferred to the Marassi prison.

A t Marassi we were split up. Our father and our brothers were taken to the section for male prisoners, and we—our mother, Maria Luisa, Bice, and I—were locked up in a large room with other women. It was a dark, dirty room. The light came in from a narrow slit, high up. The air was heavy, impossible to breathe. The four of us huddled in a corner, far from the other unfortunate women. It was easy to understand who they were by observing their behavior and, even more, by listening to their conversation, which was interrupted by brief nervous laughs. Mamma, in a low voice, told us not to look at them. My mother was literally undone by the place we were in. We had been terrified of arrest, had feared it, and within ourselves, perhaps, we had always known that, some day or other, it would happen; but the reality now, in that cell, was such as to overturn every expectation. At least, that was how it seemed to us then. The prisons of Marassi already seemed like the nightmare and yet they were only a stopping place on the way. But for us it was the first reality of the nightmare. Even more than the Casa dello Studente, where we hadn't had time to reflect, even for a moment.

At first the women were curious about us; they wanted to know who we were, and one of them said she didn't know that there was a "Jewish" crime. They insisted on speaking to us, but, faced with our silence, they ended up leaving us alone. I think they felt sorry for us.

We had put our mother in the center and we gathered close around her. I had been getting medication for a glandular abscess for some time, and now the stabbing pain became acute, but I was ashamed to mention it. Mamma suddenly remembered it, at the time when I usually took the medicine. She looked at me and held my hand.

The seven days we spent at Marassi seemed interminable to us. Inactivity and living with strangers made our state of mind worse. We endured the first humiliations. There was a single toilet hole for all the prisoners, and Maria Luisa, Bice, and I suffered above all at having to witness our mother's trauma when she had to use it. Our parents were old-fashioned, living with utter respect for modesty and convention. I don't remember ever seeing Mamma in her bathrobe or ever hearing an improper word in our house. I say this to emphasize what Mamma must have felt in those days. Our worst torment, however, was caused by our ignorance of the fate of Papa and the boys. Mamma was afraid that they had already been deported; she would go from the anguish of never seeing them again to the hope of being reunited, almost without interruption.

We tried to rouse pity in the guard who brought us food, and we persuaded him to bring us news. The next day he swore to us that the four Sonninos were still at Marassi. Our mother asked him, as if she were invoking some deity, if it was possible to bring them our greetings, and to see them. Even for a moment. The guard promised that he would do what he could. Thus, another period of waiting passed. I don't know if the promise that had been made was a way of calming us or if it truly represented that guard's kindness of heart. We saw Papa and the boys again on the evening of the seventh day of detention, when we were taken out of the room and moved to an equally squalid place, where we found our family, along with other Jews.

Papa and Giorgio looked as if they were on the verge of collapse. Giorgio threw himself into Mamma's arms and clung to her desperately. Roberto and Paolo made an effort, as usual, to appear in reasonably good spirits. There were more than a hundred people waiting to leave with us. Among them I recall Signor Della Pergola, who at one time had been the proprietor of a shoe shop in Galleria Mazzini; Signora Polacco, with two of her daughters; and a clerical worker whose name I've forgotten but who told us about himself—he was employed by a pharmaceutical company—and about his wife, from whom he had been separated. We waited for hours for the guards to come and take us. It was the middle of the night when we heard the sound of an engine in the prison yard. A truck. Women and men were separated. The Italian guards had been replaced by Germans. Hurry, hurry, they ordered us. They pushed us roughly into the back of the truck, shouting like madmen if we weren't ready and quick to obey. A few electric lights illuminated the scene. I found myself in the rear and, as I climbed over the back of the truck, I felt a sharp pain in my ankle. I fell onto a bench and had to take off one shoe; my ankle was swelling right before my eyes.

The trip from Genoa to Bolzano lasted twenty-four hours. We passed through cities and towns devastated by war; we saw long lines of people fleeing the bombardments. Kilometer upon kilometer, the chilling testimony of the war's destruction accumulated to a degree that increased our terror. The German guards checked on us from the height of the truck's cab, on which a machine gun had been placed.

On our part there was no attempt to flee. The men who could have done so—especially given their number compared with that of the guards—were restrained by the threat of reprisals against all of us if we attempted to violate the orders we had been given at our departure. I would add that, except in a few cases, members of the same family traveled in the truck and the trailer. But, even more than the fear of reprisals, I think, resignation to our destiny held us back, a sort of ancient fatalism, innate in our people. As the truck drove along, we gripped the sides or the ropes of the canvas roof as if that journey were inevitable, as if for us there could be no other. As if to be Jews meant to be slaughtered. The wind whipped faces lined with tears. But only tears. Now, in my memory, I shout to my brothers: "Save yourselves! Don't think of us!" At times I long for that memory to be reality, and in it I am as I am today and I reach out my hands to my brothers and the other Jews as if they could hear me: "Save yourselves! Don't be afraid of reprisals! Win freedom and fight for us, too!"

We arrived in Bolzano on the evening of October 20. My ankle was badly swollen. I had a hard time walking. The view of the camp was less frightening than we had expected. The seesaw of hopes and fears led us to continuously new and contradictory states of mind: we were so overwrought that, when we reached the camp, our eyes were bright and our heads were burning as if we were in the grip of a fever.

They settled us in some huts. We immediately fell into a deep sleep. Only at dawn the next day, when the guards woke us, did Mamma and we three sisters realize that we had again been separated from Papa and the boys. The sun was still low on the horizon when we were ordered to come out of the huts for the roll call. Right afterward they divided us into teams for work. Because of the condition of my ankle I was told that I could remain in the hut. Mamma, Maria Luisa, and Bice lined up with the others and were led away. I saw them going off and lay down again on the cot where I had slept. I lay without thinking, sunk in that fog that I already felt inside myself and that would become thicker and blacker until I was lost in it.

The information we gleaned that day and evening about the camp in Bolzano was scant but meaningful enough. We were told that at different points in the preceding months it had been over-crowded, and not only with Jews. It may seem strange, but it was only then that for the first time I heard talk of the partisans, of the *gappisti*,* of the resistance. Certain allusions that I had picked up from the peasants in Pietranera di Rovegno began to make sense to me: some of their secrecy, and some things that had happened in the city that at the time neither I nor the rest of my family had understood, so anxious were we to have no contact with strangers, as if it were sufficient to erect between us and others, between us and our persecutors, a barrier that would make us invisible.

Mamma, Maria Luisa, and Bice returned in the evening. Mamma was exhausted. From early morning they had been forced to work without respite in a big castle, which was probably intended to receive a German military command. Before nightfall, in spite of the weariness of Mamma and my sisters and the pain in my ankle, we left the hut and ventured as far as the perimeter fence, looking all around in fear of being discovered. Paolo and Roberto were waiting

---

* The *gappisti* were members of the G.A.P., the Partisan Action Groups, resistance groups that carried out many acts of sabotage and guerrilla warfare.

for us, without our having had to exchange a word about meeting. They knew that we would do anything to see them. We asked anxiously for news of Papa and Giorgio. Roberto begged us not to worry too much. Paolo said that, in the end, we were all alive and, in any case, we would despair when the time came. They were touching in their eagerness to instill in us even a little hope and trust.

The next day the rumor spread that a transport for Germany was being prepared. There was no roll call and work was suspended. The day was spent waiting. In the camp there was a shop where one could buy apples. In the evening, when it seemed that our departure was imminent, Mamma gathered us around her and confided to us that she had managed to conceal some money on her person, which hadn't been found even when we were searched at the entrance to the Marassi prison. She hunted in a shoe and gave us some *lire* so that we could buy apples for the journey. It was our last gift from our mother. We left the next day, in sealed freight cars. The train was escorted by a group of SS officers. A few hours after leaving Bolzano we were in German territory. It was October 23, 1944.

Traveling toward the unknown. In the car the light is faint, and gradually the air becomes impossible to breathe. The space available is so limited that we can't move. With difficulty, we manage to sit by taking turns. Among us are many elderly women, dignified women whose clothing bears obvious traces of cleanliness and elegance. They have gathered at one end of the car and talk and lament among themselves. A kind of singsong, their low voices. Among the young women I remember Eleonora Recanati Foà,* from Turin, and

* Eleonora Recanati, born in Turin March 12, 1922, was married to Guido Foà, who was killed upon arriving in Auschwitz. She was freed at Ravensbruck.

the wife of the engineer Corrado Saralvo.[*] The engineer is traveling in the car that contains the other men. Signora Saralvo suffers from a severe form of diabetes. She has a bag containing a hypodermic needle and a vial of insulin with her and from time to time she gives herself an injection. I recall another woman, I think her name was Maggi,[†] six months pregnant, obsessively preoccupied with finding a way to hide her condition from the Germans. She turns to the old women and asks them for help. No one feels like deluding her. We don't know where they are taking us. We are ignorant of the fate that awaits us, but illusions and hopes are dead.

The first day of the journey passes in the same feverish excitement that I had become familiar with in the preceding days. The second finds us tired, hungry. Little by little, relations are reduced to a few barely whispered words. Sudden outbursts of tears are frequent. The third day glints gray and yellow in

---

[*] Elena Serge, born in Turin October 26, 1904. She died in Auschwitz, date unknown.

[†] It hasn't been possible to identify this person.

the car. We have given up any formality; although we are sitting, we fall into any position. The air is foul. There isn't even a toilet hole in this tragic traveling cell. Mamma, Maria Luisa, Bice, and I are motionless for hours. Mamma sobs continuously. We embrace her tight as never before. The apples bought in Bolzano are still untouched. Like the bread they have given us. The stomach refuses food. And then there is the thought of the boys. At Bolzano we gave them part of our food ration. On the afternoon of the third day the train stops. We hear a chorus of cries coming from the men's car: "Water! Water!" A German guard slides open the door of our car and indicates to some of us to get out. My ankle hurts badly, but I can't resist and I, too, get out. We find ourselves in the middle of a plain beneath a leaden sky. Gusts of freezing wind hit us. A small abandoned house and, nearby, a fountain. The men continue to cry "Water! Water!" We fill the few containers we have with us—some cans and a tin cup—and turn to the guards. We ask if we can give water to our relatives, our brothers. The guards say yes, as long as we hurry. From the narrow opening high up ten hands reach out. For a moment, when the containers are returned, I see the faces of Paolo and Roberto. Their eyes stare at me. They disappear. The guards push us toward our car. They threaten us with the butts of their guns. We climb back in and the train departs. Those of us who got out are exhausted by the effort. On the fourth day the train stops several times. More than once we have the sensation that it's going back along the route already traveled, but probably we have lost any sense of direction. We are empty. The most precise sensation I remember is the horrible certainty of having been born, and having to live for all eternity, amid those wooden boards in motion, in that stink. My existence is a shore that grows more and more distant, almost invisible, shrouded in a thick fog. The mad desire to return there, to wake up in my bed after a night of bad dreams, fades; at times I can't even find it inside myself.

Night and cold enter through the window slit of the boxcar when the train stops yet again. We are sunk in a somnolence that has possessed us for hours—as if consciousness had been reduced to the point of forgetting oneself. This stop is lasting a long time, but we aren't paying attention. Suddenly an inferno of shouts and whistles explodes outside. It's as if a thousand dogs were barking in a battle. The doors of the cars are jerked open violently. Beams of light blind us. Soldiers in black and gray uniforms shout incomprehensible words at us. We jump to our feet, terrified. A big truck is maneuvering to approach the freight car. When it stops, the untranslatable orders multiply. A wooden plank is thrown down between the door of the car and the truck. A soldier orders a woman to move. The plank is a narrow, quivering bridge, but we must cross it. I am among the first, in the group of young women. The old women have withdrawn to the back of the car; one of them has fainted. I have time to glance at the place we're in while I struggle, with my injured ankle, to get across the plank before the tent roof of the truck onto which we are being loaded is lowered. Images that last fractions of a second. Images of eternity. In the distance, a long line of little lights, and in the fog immense pylons, like skeletons. A sea of mud, a plain of mud. A freezing, dark, muddy madness. I feel as if I had entered a dimension where nothing is human, that is utterly hostile to everything human, a dimension that has absorbed even its own creators, becoming a cold machine, muddy and dark, fatal and inexorable, topped by a small flame that I see for an instant as in the distance it breaks the darkness, as if the sky were burning: I don't yet know what it is.

The truck transports us to a large shed. We get out. We wait for the others. We wait for our brothers. Signora Saralvo asks us: "Do you think they will bring the men here, too?" The pregnant woman has her hands on her stomach as if she wished to protect what is in it. Gradually the shed grows crowded. We are at the center of the nightmare that ten years earlier had sent us its messengers. All Europe is in its power, even if by now its days are numbered.

A large bare shed. A long, interminable night. Roberto came to report to us that we are in Auschwitz. The name told us nothing. We imagine that we are in Germany and instead we are in Poland. The women are gathered at the center of the shed, pressing together in order to warm one another with the heat of their bodies. We young women often go and look outside, peering through the panes of the two windows in the wall of the shed. A wall of shadows. We can't see anything. Roberto and Paolo move from one group to the next and from time to time come and tell us what people are saying, the news that's going around. Giorgio is in our mother's lap, curled up as if he had gone back in time, as if he were asking the one who bore him to take him back into herself, to gradually eliminate him, to take away the life she has given him. Papa moves like an automaton, as if he were without senses or will. The cast on his shoulder bothers him more than ever, but he doesn't complain. Maybe he doesn't even notice it. Our sensory perceptions have collapsed. We live on the margins of consciousness. In a world absurdly unreal and real at the same time. This is the last night that my family will spend together, united. There will be no more. Eight creatures joined by bonds of blood, holding each other close for the last time.

I see my mother again, my father, my brothers, my sisters, and me, gaining, from our union, the last human warmth that is allowed us. I recall fragments of the history of my forebears. The obscure destiny within which they always struggled. For barely two generations the Sonnino and Milani families were able to be free of the humiliation of the ghetto in Rome, where the fathers of their fathers were born and grew up. The walls of the ghetto fell in 1870, and from that year the families were free. But they carried within themselves the memory of what they had endured, of anguished nights when groups of fanatics invaded the ghetto to seize their children and consecrate them, through baptism, to another religion; of the suffering caused by segregation; of the degradation they were driven to. Mamma's maternal grandmother was named Rosselli, and one day, many years earlier, I had overheard that Carlo and Nello had been killed by the Fascists, but I didn't know who they were, or what they had done.* A street in Rome, in Trastevere, where plaques recall Belli and Trilussa,† has been given the name of Crescenzio Del Monte, a first cousin of Mamma's, a poet who wrote in Judaic Roman. Aunt Ersiglia, a sister of my maternal grandfather, had married a Modigliani, a relative of the painter, and uncle Ettore Modigliani, her son, who until 1938 had

---

* Carlo Rosselli was a prominent anti-Fascist who was imprisoned and escaped to France, where, with his brother Nello, a historian, he was murdered.

† Giuseppe Gioacchino Belli (1791–1863) and Trilussa, the pen name of Carlo Alberto Salustri (1871–1950), were both poets who wrote in Roman dialect.

101

been the director of the Brera gallery, married Nelly Nathan, a niece of the mayor of Rome. Two families who had struggled hard to make lives for themselves, who had overcome the racial prejudices of certain circles of the Roman and Neapolitan bourgeoisie and earned respect. Only two generations free between the ghetto of Rome and the night of Auschwitz. A brief interlude. The wave returned to close over our heads.

The hours pass slowly in the shed. A jolt of horror when the door opens and a skeleton enters, eyes bright, wearing a striped uniform that hangs loosely on his incredibly thin body. The men crowd around. The skeleton is holding a bucket. He stops for a few moments, then with slow steps crosses the shed and disappears. Others follow. They are assigned to the camp's latrines. Night shift. One of them stops in front of me. He points to my band-aged ankle and makes a sign to take off the bandage right away. I hesitate because I don't understand. The word "selection" strikes me among others. The skeleton turns to the men and speaks agitatedly. He speaks in German. Someone translates. We must immediately remove any sign that might reveal

physical impairment. Wounds or illnesses. The selections are becoming more and more severe. The gas
chambers and the ovens are functioning non-stop.
Anyone who is unable to work is eliminated.
I immediately take off the thin paper bandage that
binds my ankle. The words seem to come not from
the mouth of a man but from the night. We beg Papa
to do the same with his cast. Papa shakes his head.
He doesn't seem to understand what we're saying.
He sinks down among us and remains motionless,
eyes closed. Mamma takes his hand and grips it.
Roberto, Paolo, Maria Luisa, Bice, and I gather
around our parents and Giorgio. We spend the rest
of the night like that, and whatever I could say of
that time, it wouldn't make sense translated into
words; it would be a thin shadow of that reality.
I would be stealing it from myself, from what is
mine, desperately mine alone.

Gray fingers at the windows of the shed signaled
that dawn had come when the SS burst in. Machine
guns raised, they array themselves around us, enclos-
ing us in a circle. Three officers, one of whom wears
the insignia of a doctor, order us to stand and line up.
As each of us is called, he takes a step forward, and

the doctor inspects, examines, tests the arm muscles. We are divided into three groups: the old, the young men, and the young women. Everything happens rapidly. We don't even have time to exchange farewells: the group of young women is the first to leave the shed amid a storm of orders shouted in a loud voice. Not even once can we turn, not a single time, to see Mamma and Papa and our brothers again. We are shoved brutally outside, into the mud that sticks to our shoes, into the freezing air. Signora Saralvo isn't with us: weeping, she told the doctor she was sick. She was added to the group of the old and the infirm.

It is October 28, 1944.

The air was foggy and cold. Desolately gray in the hallucinatory symmetry of the sheds. Shouting men and barking dogs. Commanding shrieks of whistles. The mud comes up to our ankles, thick and glue-like. Rows of phantoms in the fog, motionless, waiting, and semblances of men, leaning against one another, in the open spaces between the sheds. What awaited us when we came out of the place where we had spent the night has no reference in the human language.

My memory itself, which surely recorded it, refuses today, at a distance of fifteen years, to restore it to thought and reason. No matter how great an effort I make, the images run in rapid confusion across the screen of my mind, like a film projected too fast.

We struggled to walk, exhausted by the long journey and the lack of food, by the night in the shed, by the terror that obscured the consciousness of ourselves. Bice was between Maria Luisa and me. We won't look, we said to each other. And we pointed our eyes down at the mud, an extraordinary mud such as we had never seen before. It didn't seem like earth and water: but something organic that had decomposed, putrefied flesh that had turned liquid. And at the same time it had a presence of its own. As if death had given birth to a monstrous, vermin-like form of life, treacherous and perfidious, which grabbed us by the ankles, and kept us from moving quickly, as we had been ordered. I don't know how long we endured that torture: if we tried to raise our eyes from it, we were hurled into horror. There were twenty young women. We were led to a big shed and ordered to line up. One by one we were called to provide our personal information. After the registration, the guards ordered us to move. Another shed. They search us carefully. Nothing escapes the extremely skillful hands of the kapos. But we have nothing. The little that we brought from Bolzano remained in the place where the first selection occurred. Even the apples, which no one, not even the boys, would eat. When we go back outside, it's almost dark. A day has passed. From the tall chimneys of the crematoriums a flame rises, breaking the gray clouds and the thickening shadows. In the air is a heavy stench. We thought of our father and our mother, of our brothers. We hoped that our father and mother had been spared the mud and those sights. We couldn't imagine our father and mother victims of violence. Even today, if I try to re-create within myself the reality in which they perished, I feel my mind waver as if streams of black liquid had invaded it. That night we tried, as in the morning, not to look around us, to escape the reddish reflections of that flame.

The second day we again went from one shed-office to another for a series of further registrations whose purpose we didn't understand. Since arriving at Auschwitz we hadn't been given even a crust of bread. Only on the fourth day, after we had had showers and had our heads shaved, were we given something to eat. A few hours earlier they had tattooed the numbers on our arms: Maria Luisa A26698, me A26699, Bice A26700. A bowl of broth and a slice of black bread. Maria Luisa said we must make an effort to eat. She was about to set an example when we heard a voice behind us asking: "Are you Italian?"

We turned. A very pale, thin woman tried to smile at us. She said she was Dr. Morpurgo,* from Trieste, and asked us if we had news of a sister of hers who lived in Genoa. If she had been arrested and had traveled in the same transport with us. We answered no. The woman appeared to calm down. She asked about us. We in turn asked if there was any possibility of seeing our parents and our brothers.

---

* In all probability this is Bianca Maria Morpurgo, born in Trieste October 13, 1916, deported to Auschwitz June 30, 1944, and liberated at Leipzig. Her sister who lived in Genoa was Maura, born in Trieste March 21, 1908, and killed at Auschwitz February 6, 1944.

"Your brothers if they survive. . . . Your mother and father no. They have already been gassed."

She pointed in the direction of the chimneys, where at night the sinister flame grew red. She continued to talk to us sadly, as we wept, telling us that we must confront reality as it was, suffocating every feeling, avoiding the rise of any illusion, struggling above all to survive. She told us that it wasn't human to weep for the death of our parents: in those circumstances we should be happy that our father and mother had perished. They couldn't have a better fate. Bice seemed to have turned to ice. Maria Luisa dissolved in tears. Dr. Morpurgo stroked her hair.

Before the guards ordered her to move away she had time to tell us that we probably wouldn't stay in Auschwitz. Some sections of the camp had already been evacuated. She confirmed that the selections had become daily and were extremely rigorous. With increased sadness she concluded: "The beast has been wounded to the death and has become, if possible, more ferocious."

They locked us in Block No. 12, where we remained, waiting for our fate. If I think back to

Genoa, summer 1926. The only surviving photograph of the Sonnino siblings. From the left: Paolo,
killed at Auschwitz at the age of 27; Maria Luisa,
killed at Flossenburg at the age of 25; Giorgio, killed
at Auschwitz at the age of 19; Roberto, deceased in
an unknown place and time; Bice, killed at
Braunschweig at the age of 21; and Piera.

*When Piera Sonnino returned to Genoa she discovered the
photographs reproduced on these pages in an old chiffonier from the
house on Via Montallegro. The photographs and the chiffonier were all
that was left.*

Giorgina and Ettore Sonnino. On the back it reads:
"We want you to see us at the height of our elegance."
Naples, July 18, 1911.

Ettore Sonnino, born in Naples April 17, 1880, holding one of his daughters.

Giorgina Milani and three of her children: Giorgio (top right), Paolo, and Maria Luisa.

Maria Luisa and Bice. The last image of members of the Sonnino family before they were deported.

Maria Luisa (left) and Piera, photographed in 1934.

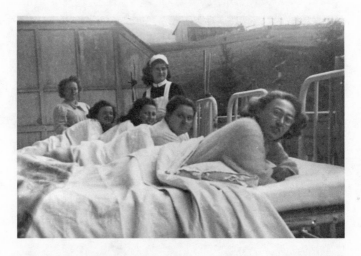

The Heliotherapy Institute Codivilla in Cortina, June 1948. It's the first photograph of Piera (front right) after her return. Carla Curti, whose testimony is quoted in Giacomo Papi's epilogue, is the second from the left.

Piera in the 1950s, after she returned to Genoa.

Above, and next two pages: Three images of Piera
after her return.

ROVEGNO · Colonia Montana · Refettorio

The Levillà Heliotherapy Colony, a kilometer from Pietranera di Rovegno, the last hiding place of the Sonninos before they returned to Genoa. The colony was first in the hands of the Nazi-Fascists and then from 1944 it was a prison and operation base for the partisans. For years after the war, dead bodies of soldiers were recovered in the neighboring woods.

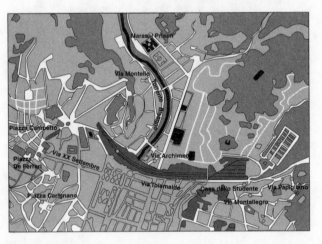

Map of Genoa.

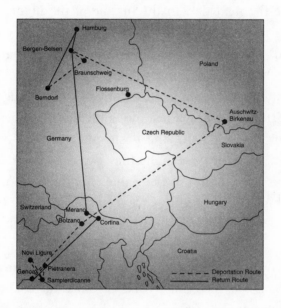

Map of the deportation route of the Sonnino family,
and Piera's return to Genoa.

those days, in my memory I find only night. Darkness. As if my mind were paralyzed.

A few days later the news spread that we would leave the next day. In the middle of the night they woke us for the roll call. We were crowded into a bare open space where darkness loomed, canceling out all light, except the obsessive red flame of the chimneys. To endure the cold we tried to take refuge in the strangest and wildest thoughts. But the frigid air penetrated the skin, the flesh, plunging the brain into a deep torpor. Finally they gave us the order to move. In a column we walked in that darkness, without knowing where we were headed. The livid dawn found us lined up beside a train. We got into the cars and the German guards closed the doors heavily behind us. As the train began its journey, Maria Luisa, Bice, and I tried to glance at Auschwitz one last time: our parents and our brothers were there. In our hearts was the unconfessable hope that, in spite of everything, in spite of what we had seen and learned, Mamma and Papa were still alive, that we would see them again, together with Paolo, Roberto, and Giorgio.

That two-day journey has no story. We were all at the limits of our strength. We lay on top of one another without moving, without speaking. Hunger, after a period of spasmodic intensity, seemed to diminish. To me it seemed I no longer had a stomach. No longer had a shape. No past and no future. Yet I was conscious that that was only the beginning. We could measure, in the fearful living skeletons of our companions, the sufferings that still awaited us.

When the train halted and, after a long delay, the doors of the cars were reopened, we had the sensation of having returned to the place we had started from.

In front of us was the night, a foggy, cold night, and a sea of mud. The barracks that confronted us seemed to have emerged from the dreams of a madman: permeated by a stench that took away your breath, with triple-decker bunks attached to one another, and inhabited by phantoms. We crowded in, trying only to keep each other warm. As we crossed the camp one of us had asked where we were.

"Belsen" had been the response.

The next morning, at dawn, the roll calls began outside, in the freezing air of a harsh winter. We experienced the depths of cruelty. For a foolish mistake made during work Maria Luisa was beaten till she bled before our eyes, mine and Bice's. Every morning when we came out of the huts, the guards urged us to move more quickly, hitting us one by one with a stick or with a whip. Our bodies were covered with bruises. At night before we went to sleep, the next day's waking seemed to us a nightmare.

A month after our arrival, we left Belsen. Maria Luisa, Bice, and I, with a Jewish woman from Trieste whose name I don't remember, two from Lodi, Eleonora Recanati Foà from Turin, and Noemi Jona,[*] from Rome, joined seven hundred Hungarian Jews and were transferred to a camp near Braunschweig. I don't remember how long the journey lasted. Nor the conditions under which we made it. The gaps in my mind become more and more prolonged. At Braunschweig we were lodged in a stable where there was room for three hundred at most. A single tap had to do for all. The latrine was a stinking hut of uneven wooden boards. Every morning at dawn we crossed the city to the neighborhoods that had

---

[*] Born Foà in Castagnole Lanze, Asti, February 14, 1908, and liberated at Ravensbruck.

been damaged by bombs. Maria Luisa, Bice, and I, when we could, walked holding each other by the hand. Bice was very weak and, since the end of our stay in Belsen, had had a bad case of dysentery. Maria Luisa was the one who was most resistant. She was thin and her breasts and hips had disappeared, but her brain and her nerves were sufficiently solid. Many times she tried to sing for us, to instill hope and faith. She was more than our sister. In the end Bice and I saw her as our mother. In the morning, as we went to work, she even tried to distract us, pointing out now a building, a tree, some object. Often the passersby threw rocks at us or someone shoved his way into our midst to spit on us. But we experienced also the other side of Germany, the real one, the one not corrupted by Hitlerism. One morning, after several hours of work, Maria Luisa became faint. She fell down among the rubble that she was shoveling. Bice and I, desperate with fear that the snow and the cold would make our sister's condition worse, helped her get up and sheltered her in a doorway. We had been there for a few minutes, divided between worry that the guards would discover our absence and the even greater anxiety that

Maria Luisa would get sicker, when the door that we had half closed opened. A German entered, an old woman with a crown of white hair above her face, holding a thermos. She made a sign that it was for Maria Luisa. The hot tea revived our sister. The woman took some bread from a pocket of the apron that she wore under her heavy coat and divided it into three pieces. She went away with a look in which we found something of what we had lost. Returning to work, we could just see her behind the panes of a window in the building opposite the one that the bombs had destroyed.

Eleonora Recanati Foà also found Germans who helped her. She was suffering from a sore on one leg that threatened to become infected. She got the medicine that she needed either in a pharmacy or in a private house—I don't know which—near our workplace. The supervisors, however, were aware of her absences and of what was happening.

At Braunschweig we also met some Italian civilians. They were assigned to excavation work, and every morning they distributed picks and shovels. They had never seen people who had been deported to the extermination camps. They were terrified by our larva-like aspect. When they found out that there were some Italians among the Hungarians, they looked for us. They, too, were in a difficult situation, and hadn't enough food. Every morning, using every possible ruse, they tried to slip pieces of bread into our hands along with the tools, sometimes as small and thin as a mouthful. All they had. When they had nothing to give us, they waited for us with a sad expression on their faces. They also tried to help us with regard to our clothing. We were nearly naked and unprotected from the severe winter. Our hands were cracked and bleeding. They couldn't do much, but they gave us gloves, although mismatched, and pieces of blankets and old clothes to protect ourselves as well as we could. They gave Bice a blue hood that covered her head and went down over her neck. It was early January of 1945.

One night, when we returned to the barracks, a guard came and read a list of names: first Hungarians and then two Italians. One of them was Maria Luisa. The order to assemble was so sudden that Maria Luisa had to run. We thought that hours of night work awaited her and we suffered for her, already so tired from the long day. In the morning, upon awaking, we were sure from one moment to the next that we would see her; in fact, as we opened our eyes, we counted on finding her beside us, having returned during the night. In the evening, Bice and I couldn't wait to reach the stable. Maria Luisa still wasn't there. One of the Hungarians made us understand that, with the others, she had gone to a camp far from ours. That night, Bice and I wept desperately, hugging each other.

After Maria Luisa's departure, Bice began to get worse. She cried often and complained. She was visibly losing her strength. Her eighteen years seemed to be contracted, almost crumpled, she was like a leaf torn, still green, from a tree, lying in the dust in the sun. She was becoming a creature without age, pale with that papery white pallor of the "subhumans." She had grown feeble and she moved slowly, as if every gesture cost her infinite effort. As long as Maria Luisa was there, we were two to help her; then I was alone. Alone I dragged her along the road that led to work, alone

I protected her from the guards, alone I tried to prevent her from getting the harder jobs, alone I strove to maintain life in her. And I, too, found myself completing the most elementary gesture as if it were terribly complicated and difficult. I discovered that I was without flesh, skin stretched over bones.

What I mainly managed to do was to stay beside her, to never lose sight of her. I suffered at night because we slept apart, Bice among the Hungarians, next to a wooden beam that had once held a stove or work equipment, and I against a wall of the stable.

On the night of January 13 Bice complained more than usual on the way back. Her dysentery was continuous, unstoppable; there was no position that moderated it even for a moment. At work, on the road, on her bed. That night my sister, after the first spoonful of broth, had a bout of vomiting; she pushed away her bowl and threw herself on her filthy pallet. I stayed with her until the Hungarians ordered me away. I intended to remain awake to hear if Bice cried out, but I was so exhausted that I fell immediately into a deep sleep. At dawn, as usual, the guards woke us shouting and waving sticks. I ran to Bice: her eyes were open and staring at the ceiling. I had the sensation that she hadn't slept. I tried to raise her so that she could get up. The guards in the yard outside were already announcing the roll call. Bice tried to help my efforts, but she fell back heavily. I urged her. It was in vain. I ran desperately out of the stable.

A guard threatened me with a stick. I wept as I tried to make her understand that Bice was too sick to work that day. The guard hurled herself at me like a fury. She beat me and I went on crying, she hit me on the head, in the face, on the chest, and I went on crying, screaming, I didn't feel the pain of the blows, I felt nothing: there is no trace of them in me, there is only the anguish of anticipating that I would not make myself understood, that the guard would enter the stable and beat Bice, too. I managed to grab the woman by an arm and drag her inside. Finally the guard understood what I was saying. She leaned over Bice, gave her a rapid glance, then, with a gesture of disgust, sent me out. My sister stayed there, lying on the straw pallet, while I, lining up with the others, went to work. The day was agonizingly long. It's difficult to find words to describe how the measure of time is simply a convention, how there exists within us a time that can contract and expand infinitely, escaping any calculation. When evening came I was more exhausted by waiting than by the work.

Bice was in the same position in which I had left her that morning. Near her was a bowl half full of soup and a piece of bread. As soon as she saw me come in she indicated both with a small nod of her head. Her head was wrapped in her blue hood.

I looked at her and for an instant fear and hope clashed within me. Bice's face was relaxed, her eyes almost clear. I asked her how she was. For the first time in many days, she said that she was very well. I asked a Hungarian woman for permission to sleep beside my sister. I didn't even get an answer. The woman fell almost diagonally on her pallet and closed her eyes. I tried to resist sleep. I knew that I shouldn't sleep. But weariness was stronger than will.

That sleep was only a rapid closing and opening of my eyes. The night, from darkness to dawn, lasted a moment. I awoke to the shouts of the guards. Bice was motionless, her eyes still open in that strange stare. The straw under her and around her was rotted because of the dysentery. In a whisper she persisted in telling me that she was well. She seemed to have reached a state in which there was no more suffering. At the end of the roll call I prostrated myself before the guard who had beaten me the day before, I asked her to let me stay with my sister. I repeated the word "death," the only word I had learned in German. I was kneeling in front of that woman, with my head bowed so that my forehead touched the ground. The stick came down on my shoulders and I felt a pain in my chest. Mamma, Mamma . . . I called. Mamma, Mamma . . . help me. Bice is dying, make this woman understand, make her have a crumb of humanity. I was still bent over, face to the ground, when I heard the steps of the column moving into the distance. I ran to Bice like a madwoman.

Bice didn't even ask me why I hadn't gone to work. I took her hand and held it tight. A little later I thought it would be good to clean her bed and wash her. I held her lovingly under her arms and was about to lift her up when a long rattle paralyzed me. I laid her down again and took her hand. I stayed like that all day, without moving, without speaking, with the absurd hope of transmitting warmth and life to that body. I knew what was about to happen, but I wouldn't believe it. Bice was the last solid fragment of the past that remained to me. With growing fear I felt how the absences of my mind were becoming longer and longer, the giving in more frequent, the will to live ever weaker. I knew those symptoms because others had often spoken about them and I knew what they meant. Yet as long as Bice was with me I knew also that I would not let myself be crushed. But the sparks kindled in me for my own fate were fleeting: I was too absorbed in Bice's.

Again I saw my sister as a child, yet again I glimpsed her growing serious and calm like our mother, incapable of showing or nourishing any resentment, generous. Bice was the fragment of a past made up of anxiety and fear, but also of affection. We went to school together, and were called "the artichoke sisters," a nickname that sometimes made us laugh. Artichokes, because we were sharp and prickly. We said to our schoolmates: We would like to invite you to our house, but how can we? Everything is a mess. We're putting the house in order. An order that would take the entire school year to achieve. If someone persisted, we became, without intending it, rude. My father's bad luck and then, after 1938, his financial ruin and premature old age; and us, his daughters, trying to distract him, to rouse the lighthearted spirit of long ago— thousands and thousands of images of our house, of our family were around me and Bice that day. And perhaps Bice didn't recall them as images but lived them as reality. Maybe she had returned home from a long trip and had knocked at the door and Mamma had opened it and we had all come to greet her and embrace her and kiss her. None of us spoke of perse- cution, of flight; the sky was blue, and the blue and green light flooded in from the garden of our house. Giorgio was dancing with Bice and we were clapping our hands and Bice no longer remembered what had happened. Not even that she had left and returned. A gap of time was closed up, the edges were sealed, expelling the evil, and for Bice perhaps life began again in the years when the messengers of the night- mare had not yet reached us. Maybe for this reason Bice said that she was well and lay there without moaning anymore, her face, white as paper, relaxed.

When the Hungarians returned I had to leave my sister. I am ashamed to write it, but that night, too, although I used all my strength to resist, I fell asleep. I woke suddenly, oppressed by a sensation of terror. Dawn was near. I called Signora Foà, I begged her to come and see how Bice was. She struggled to get up, still sleepy. She climbed over the bodies of the other women, who groaned in their sleep, and reached Bice's bed. She leaned over it and was still for a moment. I saw her reach out a hand to touch my sister. I closed my eyes. Mamma, Mamma . . . I implored her. Signora Foà came back and placed a hand on my head. She's dead, she said in a murmur.

Beside Bice, I witnessed the breaking of a gray snowy day. In the course of the morning a kapo came to ask me for information about my sister. She recorded everything with extreme diligence. She went away without a glance at that lifeless body. In the afternoon they came to take the body. They carried it out of the stable and placed it on a bench near the door of the latrine. It was snowing. They threw over my sister a sack that barely covered her flattened stomach. Her face, encircled by the blue hood, was exposed to the snow, as were her hands and legs. The next morning, before the roll call, during the time when we were allowed to go to the latrine, I went past Bice. I went past again in the evening, and the next day and evening, and again the day after and yet another day. After four days very little of Bice emerged from under the snow. And from that moment my memories become confused, detached, impersonal. My subconscious holds them like an evil nesting inside me. I know that I should free myself of them but I cannot. I am not capable of bringing them to the surface of consciousness.

I remember that at the end of March, along with Signora Foà, Noemi Jona, the Jewish woman from Trieste, and a group of Hungarians, I was transferred to another camp. To Berndorf.* I'm not sure that this is the exact name: it's a name I heard without ever having seen it written. At Berndorf there was an underground factory that made airplane parts. In the tunnels the air was soft, and it was warm; after the cold we had endured working among the ruins of Braunschweig, that warmth welcomed us like summer. I have an animal memory of it, as of a pleasure in which the mind did not participate in any degree. Signora Foà was assigned to a different

---

* The reference is to Bendorf am Main, near Koblenz.

shift from mine. I stayed with the woman from Trieste: two Italians among a hundred Hungarians. The woman from Trieste was so thin that it was frightening to look at her. I recall that one night it seemed that she was going to give up, abandon life. When that happened, death was near. She held me close and whispered in my ear that she had been arrested because of her stepmother, who had reported her. My father must know it, she repeated. He must know it. The next day she rose in a daze and took up the usual existence. After a few days she disappeared. I never saw her again.

In that period, in a stupid accident, I broke my eyeglasses. It was as if I had become blind. The world contracted around me. It was transformed into hazy and evanescent shapes; everywhere were threats and dangers. I was alone and blind. In my mind at this point there is a void that I can't even try to fill, because I know it would be impossible. The void is interrupted. We are lined up and we cross Berndorf in a mad run. They push us into a railroad car. They close the door. The train moves. I have no sense of the direction. Again an absence. When the train stops and the door opens I have a confused glimpse of some of us taking bodies and rolling them out. This is repeated often. I wake up on something soft and hard at the same time. I touch it. There are legs, it's a stomach, it's a bed. A face. Frozen. I have slept on a dead woman. Again a void. Choruses of cries like a furious, wailing wind. I no longer know if the images of my memory are fragments of reality— it's unthinkable that it can have recorded the whole reality—or hallucinations. The train stops again, we have to get out, help those who cannot get out. Two Hungarians take me by the arms, a short distance away I see the chaotic mass of our companions gathered in a square, I regain consciousness and find my mouth in the dust, thirst torments me, I look around, the square has become an endless plain, I am alone, I get up crying, terrified, and begin to run, a barrel of rainwater, I lean over to drink, the water is dirty, fear that it might be harmful assails me, but I continue to drink, then start running again, a wall in front of me, a barracks, someone who lays me down on a straw pallet and then nothing more.

The memories of the following days are also jumbled. From the pallet on which I was lying I could make out through the windowpanes piles of crates and khaki uniforms, and a confusion of shouts reached my ears; suddenly the roar of engines drowned out every other noise, a roar that remained in my mind for a long time. My body ached and I had a high fever. I was incapable of any movement or any thought.

I was aware of the presence of other women beside me in the same hut, but I couldn't say who or how many they were. The veil of unconsciousness tears when a voice announces that the next day I will be moved to the hospital. Terror shakes me: I scream. I don't want to go to the hospital. I know what going to the hospital means. I don't want to be gassed. I try to get up to demonstrate how well I am. I can work, of course I can, I am standing up, I wave my arms, I don't need any treatment. I again lose consciousness of myself and of time. Another image: the next day. Two men enter with a stretcher and come toward me. I start screaming again. I grip the edges of the pallet, the sheets. I'm not sick, I'm perfectly well. I feel strong. I've never been so full of energy. For pity's sake, spare me. The two men are near me. I call on Mamma, Roberto, Paolo to come and protect me, to keep those men from taking me away. I have the impression that I am fighting like a wild beast to save my life and yet with no effort the two men lift me up and load me onto the stretcher. I continue to scream. All my senses are painfully acute. The ambulance moves. A broad staircase. White corridors. A bed. I fall again into unconsciousness. A cool hand on my forehead. I open my eyes. A nurse is leaning over me.

"How are you?" she asks in Italian.

My first thought is shaken by waves of terror.

"I'm fine. I can work. Let me get up. I'm going right to work."

The nurse doesn't understand. I remember her face leaning over, almost touching mine.

"I'm asking you how you feel!"

I burst into tears.

"You're Italian, like me," I sob, "please let me get out of here. Let me go back to the barracks. I can work. I don't want to be gassed."

The nurse's eyes widen. In that dark twilight of my mind I see them become big, enormous. Full of rain. Two arms embrace me and a breast welcomes my shaved head, the skull that is my face.

The nurse begins to speak. Each word brings me slowly back to life. It's May 17, she tells me. The war has been over for nine days. You are in the hospital of Altona, in Hamburg. You came here on May 9. I try to rouse myself. No, I say, it's impossible. The war isn't over. Tell me the truth, don't deceive me. Tell me instead that I have to die. The nurse strokes my head. The war is over, she insists. She leaves me for a moment. She returns with cigarettes, choco- late, American cookies, she scatters them on my bed. I begin to laugh. Good, the nurse applauds, yes. Yes. Look around. See how clean it is. This morning you seemed awake when the doctors came to see you. Tell me, would the Germans send so many doctors to see you? Do you believe now that the war is over? I laugh, I believe it, I believe it. Let me get up. Let me go home. Maybe my family is already on the way to Italy. My family. A cloud. The nurse gives me something to drink. Be quiet now, she whispers. Try to sleep. You are sick. Very sick. But you won't die and you will be able to go home. Like your family.

August 26, a great day. With other Italians I leave the hospital in Hamburg on a stretcher. The nurse comes to say goodbye. In a couple of days you will be home. A hospital train is waiting in the station. The train leaves almost immediately. A deep, obscure happiness pervades me and almost feeds the hope of finding my family. My mind is still so weak that I name them and think of them all: Papa, Mamma, Roberto, Giorgio, Maria Luisa, Bice . . . even Bice. Only at times a dark memory troubles me. A bench and on it a pile of snow. The leaden sky.

After a few hours the train stops. The Red Cross nurses go from car to car: those who are able to make a short trip get ready. The others will spend the night on the train. The next day, still on the stretcher, I am carried off the train. The sight that greets my eyes overpowers my mind; I lose that tiny equilibrium of nerves that I had managed to gain. We are looking at the huts in the camp at Belsen. I don't know why the hospital train that left for Italy has been forced to make this stop, I don't know why the American authorities, who had been so generous, found the need to impose on us this last torture, but I have only to close my eyes to feel the collapse of my reason and my strength in the face of what I was seeing again. The stay in Belsen extended to the middle of September. The Americans did not spare any effort, employing all their knowledge to restore us to life, to revive our will to live. I used that time in a desperate search, through the Red Cross and some deportees from the former camp, for any trace of Maria Luisa. I thought that from Braunschweig she had been sent back to Belsen, but all my searching was in vain.

Finally, on September 21, 1945, I see Italy again. The moment we crossed the border the train was a single shout. It was our life that, having escaped extermination, shouted, cried, went wild.

147

I was admitted to the Red Cross hospital in Merano. I immediately wrote to my relatives to say that I had returned. On October 1 a nurse came rushing, out of breath, to tell me that I had a visitor. I left my bed and, just as I was, ran out: in the shadowy light of the corridor I saw coming toward me someone I thought I recognized. An uncontrollable impulse filled my heart and my throat: "Roberto! Roberto!" I shouted. My eyes were full of tears and it wasn't until he had got very close that I knew he wasn't Roberto. It was Carlo, the son of Uncle Flavio. I asked Carlo anxiously for news of my family. My cousin answered me sorrowfully that he had none. So far, only I had communicated that I had survived. But I mustn't despair, Carlo added. The repatriations were far from over.

I wrote immediately to the Ministry for Postwar Aid. On November 9 the first response arrived. "We are very sorry to have to inform you that on the lists up to now in our possession appears a Signorina Maria Luisa Sonnino, born October 5, 1920, deceased in Flossenburg March 20, 1945: we are afraid it is the sister you were looking for. Further, on a list sent to us by the Jewish Community of Milan 'the Sonnino family of Genoa' appears as deceased, without other details, this last information brought by Mr. Giuseppe Mortara of Bologna."

It wasn't until three years later, on September 29, 1948, that I had any news of the end of my brothers. The engineer Simone Spritmann, who was on our transport from Bolzano to Auschwitz, sent me a letter, from which I quote some passages:

On the night, or rather the morning, of October 28, 1944, in the salone at Saune, as we were lined up and a lieutenant of the SS was walking down our row, I was next to your older brother. I recall this very well. He complained during the interrogation of being bothered by the aftereffects of pleurisy. He was put in the group where his father was. Of Roberto I can say little. To me it seems that he went on the transport.* He soon disappeared from circulation. Giorgio, however, poor dear, gentle Giorgio, was with me for a long time. He was like a son. I had to struggle with him, I confess that I even had to hit him. That boy was giving up. He

*   To the gas chamber.

wouldn't resist. He wouldn't even line up for his ration. For a long time I was mainly the one who helped him. This was as long as we remained in the same shed and the same job. Reproaches, jokes, nothing, nothing availed. He slowly let go until the move to Krankenbau. This happened around the end of November. I never saw him again.

The ashes of my mother, my father, Paolo, Roberto, and Giorgio are in Auschwitz. Maria Luisa ended up in a common grave. As for Bice, I don't know where she was buried.

In May of 1946 I left the hospital in Merano and was transferred to the clinic in Loano, run by Professor Zanoli, where I stayed until May 1948. On June 1 of that year I was admitted to the Instituto Codivilla, in Cortina, from which I was discharged in September 1950. My uncle Flavio Sonnino, my father's brother, did not spare any expense to make sure that I got the best possible care.

These were years of complete indifference, lived passively, in a solitude without end. I was often very ill. I had pleurisy many times, and I was forced to stay in bed for months; for a long time, even after leaving the hospitals, I had to wear a corset to combat spondylitis. What remained of the life force survived, perhaps, only in the fact that I surrendered to every type of treatment. Often I was seized by fits of weeping that left me stunned. More than once I caught myself wishing to die; the wish to die was always present in me but as something natural, not intense or painful. In Merano, Loano, and then Cortina, I met people, men and women who were sick like me, patients in the same rest homes as me, but I couldn't form deep friendships. It was as if I were still among the Hungarian Jews and unable to communicate.

On September 21, 1950, after six years of absence, I set foot again in Genoa. What can I say of that return? Of being in the city that I had dreamed of and desperately yearned for, that seemed to me my home and that I had found again, but empty of those I loved? My aunt Anna and my cousin Giulia, the wife of a nephew of my father, were waiting for me. Also waiting were the streets, the squares, the places where I had lived with my brothers and sisters, a reality that now existed without them but that I was part of. They were days of an unforgettable intensity. Of a grief renewed to its roots. When I could, I tried to discover the fate of what we had left in the house on Via Montallegro. The apartment had been completely ransacked and emptied. Of all that we possessed I managed to recover a single piece of furniture, an old chiffonier. Some time afterward, having learned of my return, a woman who lived on Via Montallegro brought me something that she had found in the dust the day the house was looted: a photograph of my mother, the only one I possess of her last years.

I spent some months with my aunt Anna and then my life took a turn. I met some men and women with whom I realized I could get along. It wasn't easy for me to overcome the barrier that divided me from them. But when I did I found myself as if in a new world: a world of simple, optimistic people, profoundly serious and conscious of the value of human life, of the rights of the human character, of human feelings. It was thanks to them that

I began to see clearly into myself and into the story of my family; thanks to them if I found myself, many times, in front of a microphone, speaking in a voice that, though it was uncertain, held all my sorrow and all my hopes: "Companions, friends, brothers, let us all work together so that no family on earth may ever experience my long night of Auschwitz, the long night of the martyrdom of my people and of all European peoples. . . ."

Epilogue

Giacomo Papi

GIACOMO PAPI is a journalist at *Diario*, the Italian newsmagazine that first published Sonnino's memoir, and the author of *Booked*. Together with Massimo Coppola, he runs ISBN Edizioni, an imprint of the Italian book publisher Saggiatore.

Sixty typewritten pages, without an error, without a correction. Reconsidered, rewritten, refined, to be preserved for forty-two years in a red leather binder. The memories were an invisible presence in the house. They were the shadow that disappeared into a drawer and reappeared years later, whenever the family moved, only to vanish again. A text so complete that it is difficult to understand why it wasn't published at the time. Perhaps, when Piera Sonnino returned to Genoa in September 1950, at the age of twenty-eight, she couldn't put her memories in order. First she had to try to live.

She met Antonio Gaetano Parodi, Communist, playwright, and journalist for *l'Unità*. They married almost immediately. In 1954 Bice was born, in 1959 Maria Luisa. The diary was finished the following year. With a date: "Genoa, July 1960," the very year and month in which the city, which had received a Gold Medal of the Resistance, rose up in protest to prevent the Movimento Sociale Italiano, the revived neo-Fascist party, from holding its annual convention there. Scheduled to preside over the convention was the former prefect of Genoa, Carlo Emanuele Basile, the man who had welcomed the Nazis to the city and unleashed the persecution of the Jews.

The way in which Piera Sonnino, from her first words, weighs her sentences, calibrates her adjectives, and the way in which, before beginning to reconstruct a particular series of events, she evaluates her own capacity to remember, offers a great lesson in memory as a privilege of man, as a privilege of those who are still human beings. In the effort to put events in order, even when memory fails and everything appears too horrifying to be believed, Sonnino succeeds in describing, by repeating them to herself, those characteristics of modesty, dignity, and shame that kept her family from putting up even the most tenuous resistance. This sense of propriety can be transformed into resignation, into silence and immobility. This is the nucleus of the Sonnino family's behavior, as, fleeing Genoa, it kept making increasingly smaller circles, coming ever closer to the source of danger. The most classic of bourgeois values is accentuated by the travertine smile that Fascism required of everyone. Sonnino notes this, too: "The official optimism of the regime did not admit or tolerate economic catastrophe. . . . I think that this, in the end, even if we were unconscious of it, in some way legitimized what we considered dignity and decorum." In the case of the Sonnino family, the sense of propriety slipped into timidity, and became surrender. Sonnino's daughter Maria Luisa recalls: "When, as small children, we made a fuss, a typical phrase of Mamma's was: 'Children, let's not make a spectacle of ourselves.' " Not to be a spectacle—not to be noticed—was the only strategy that the Sonninos, and many who shared their tragedy, managed to develop in the face of the advancing horror.

In 2002, *Diario*, the weekly I work for, embarked on a project entitled *La Memoria Lunga* (A long

memory). The idea came from two readers—Juri
Guida and Andrea Lilli. It was a simple idea: invite
readers to send a memory of their grandparents, in
order to preserve an episode that would otherwise be
lost. On May 17, 2002, an e-mail arrived: "My name
is Maria Luisa Parodi. I am the daughter of Piera
Sonnino, a survivor of the Shoah who died three
years ago. My mother wrote a diary, which my sister
and I have kept private for a long time. Now it is time
(and I assure you that letting go of it required a personal journey that was and is painful), if you consider
it appropriate, to make it public and share it." A few
days later, the manuscript arrived at the office. It was
entitled "The Night of Auschwitz," a title that may
appear banal today but that in 1960, two years after
the publication of Primo Levi's *If This Is a Man*,
included a word—Auschwitz—that had not yet
become overused. It was published in its entirety in
the special issue that *Diario* devotes to the Day of
Remembrance, January 27.

———————

If you look up over the tollbooth on the highway at
Chiavari, you can see a house, the first refuge of the

Sonnino family when they left Genoa. It's a three-story villa, falling down now, that stands beside the town cemetery. No one has lived there for decades, and the lawn is a forest of weeds. When the deportation of the Italian Jews began, the Sonnino family was living here. Sampierdicanne, which was then a "little town a few kilometers from Chiavari," has been completely absorbed by the city. The few houses and the church are literally overhung by the concrete pillars and the overpass of the highway.

Maria Sanguineti still lives here. She is a kind woman, widowed many years ago. At the time of the events of the book she was a girl. Her aunt and uncle were tenant farmers of the Castagnola family, wealthy landowners in Chiavari who had rented the villa to the Sonninos. She showed me a black-and-white photograph taken in the sixties. Two old people, slightly bent, stand smiling at the top of the steps leading to the entrance of the house. It's this man, probably, who was the "poor peasant of Sampierdicanne," for whom "humanity is divided not between Jews and non-Jews but between rich and poor, between those who possess everything and those who possess nothing." Maria Sanguineti pointed to a stone seat to the right of the door. She said that Giorgio, the youngest of the brothers, loved to sit there with the gramophone and records and call together all the children of the town to come and listen to the music. "They were the popular songs of the time. I recall that he often played 'La Piemontese,' because my aunt liked it." She sang it:

> Farewell lovely days of the past
> I have to leave you, my dear friend,
> My studies are over,
> So our dream has ended
> I am going far away, I don't know where
> I leave with regret in my heart
> Give me one last kiss.

She said that he was a nice boy. One of his admonitions impressed her in particular: "He always said to us: 'Pray to the Lord, children.' I asked my aunt why he always said the Lord and never Jesus. She explained to me that Giorgio and his family didn't believe in Jesus because they were Jews." Sanguineti remembered "the one with the glasses," that is, Piera, and the mother, "because she was fat, in contrast with the aunt, who was tall and thin." She went on, "A short time after they left, the Germans arrived.

They camped on the field opposite the house—they
must have been two hundred meters away as the
crow flies. . . . They would have arrested them even
if they had stayed here." The tragedy of the Sonninos
may look like a succession of wrong moves. If you
examine the situation more closely, you realize how
slim their chances for safety were, no matter what
they might have done.

From September 8 to the end of the war, the road
that connects Chiavari to Alta Val Trebbia represented one of the nerve centers of the war of liberation. The first nucleus of the Resistance in Liguria
was formed in Favale, just inland from Chiavari. For
nineteen months, on both sides, that road was the
scene of roundups, shootings, violence, summary
executions. Partisans, Nazis, Fascists, even Mongol
soldiers allied with the Germans moved about those
mountains, won and lost positions, procured food.
The nine members of the Sonnino family (Aunt
Anna was always with them) traveled along this road
at the end of September 1943 to get to Pietranera di
Rovegno. Even today people here can point out a
mountain, Mount Carmo, and relate how until the
sixties the southern slope was lushly green because

of the dead who, abandoned on the ridge, enriched the earth. By 1944 there were some four thousand partisans in the area, but in the autumn of 1943 they were not so many. On the enemy front, there were the Germans and their Mongol and Turkish troops, and the Fascist brigades, for a total of almost ten thousand soldiers. In a certain sense, it was the worst place to try to hide.

It has not been possible to find out the name of the marshal of the *carabinieri* who in November 1943, instead of proceeding to arrest the Sonninos, asked them to leave. According to Antonio Testa's book *Partigiani in Val Trebbia*, this marshal was a man of "declared Fascist orientation." One's impression is that the strategy of invisibility that the Sonninos had adopted had also blinded them, made them incapable of understanding what was happening around them and of recognizing the possibilities of safety that were open to them. If they had known of the presence of the partisans (and from Sonnino's account it doesn't seem that they did), if they had just allowed themselves to hope that Nazi-Fascism would soon be defeated, the men could have joined the Resistance. The women would have had a better chance of hiding.

Pietranera is a village of fewer than a hundred inhabitants, thirty houses on a road halfway up the mountain, a couple of miles from Rovegno. Old people in the only restaurant and on the street seemed to know about the Sonnino family, and many remember them. *That's the house where they stayed, the three-story white one, where the town begins. In those days it was a kind of inn. Now the children of the proprietor live there. But they ate somewhere else, in a room that a peasant rented to them. In that house over there, on the ground floor. The door was where you see that window. Now it has been walled up.* Everyone knew that the family hadn't survived, but in a vague way, as with news heard too quickly. Silvio Mazzoni, a carpenter, was a child. A single detail impressed itself in his memory: "I have a clear memory only of the father, because he made cigarettes with chamomile."

Aldo Muzio, his neighbor, interrupted: "And in fact there was always an odor of chamomile in the air. We boys often went to their house, in the afternoon, to listen to music. It was the youngest, Giorgio, it seems to me, who put records on the gramophone. Imagine, for us who barely had anything to eat. . . ."

That gramophone, the focus of memories here, too, as in Sampierdicanne, was probably the last whimsical gesture of Ettore Sonnino.

"There were three sisters, I think," Muzio continued. "I recall that the youngest, Bice, was the most reserved. She would keep to herself while we listened to the current popular songs. The others were all very sociable. I became friends with the two older brothers, especially Paolo, maybe because he had a degree in business and economics, the faculty where I was enrolled. Before the summer I had taken a diploma in bookkeeping. I recall that we talked mainly about our studies."

I asked if he remembered anything about the Sonninos' departure from the village, to return to Genoa and be sent to death. Aldo Muzio answered:

At the time the partisan struggle was in an early phase, and it's possible that they didn't know anything about it. After the visit to the *carabinieri* in Rovegno, I remember that we went around to the neighboring villages with Roberto and Paolo to try to find a place to hide. We went to Alpe Piana, a tiny town that is just over the mountain. I remember that once, on the way back, we completely lost our way. It grew dark, and we didn't know where we were or where we were going. Luckily, at some point a rooster crowed, so we walked in that direction. We arrived in Foppiano, another town nearby, and from there we managed to get back to Rovegno. A few days later I accompanied them to Barchi, in the community of Gorreto. My father was born there, so we decided to see if a cousin was willing to take them in, but it wasn't possible. You have to understand, they were nine people and no one here had anything to eat. How could we help them?

Too paralyzed to perceive—and to comprehend—the direction that history was taking, the Sonnino family returned to Genoa. It was early December 1943. In the diary the moment of their return is described thus: "We had returned to the point of departure. We found ourselves, with the few things we had brought from Pietranera, in an unknown place, on the threshold of a city that was no longer ours, that appeared to us an enormous trap to which, ineluctably, we were condemned to return." What Piera Sonnino calls "the influence of the magic family circle, and the place we were used to" finds a geographic parallel in the circuit that the family makes, returning, in the end, to the very street where Ettore Sonnino and Giorgina Milani settled in 1925, with six small children, when they moved from Milan to Genoa. "Our story, which had practically begun on that street, would end on the same pavement, within the same walls, in the same setting." The windows of some of the buildings on Via Montallegro are less than thirty meters from those of the Casa dello Studente, the headquarters of the Nazi-Fascist central command, where prisoners were brought before being sent to Germany, tortured, or killed. It is unlikely that the house where they settled was one of these. It is more likely that it was at the other end of the street (in the part that today is called Via Maurizio Sacchi). In any case, not more than eight hundred meters from the entrance to the Casa dello Studente.

The family arrived in Auschwitz on October 28, 1944. The ovens were operating non-stop. Of the 196 men who traveled on Piera's train, only 59 were tattooed, the rest were sent immediately to the gas chambers. Among them was Ettore, her father, and Paolo, her oldest brother, who during the selection made the mistake of declaring that he had had pleurisy. For Roberto and Giorgio it was another month or a little more. The engineer Corrado Saralvo, who traveled from Bolzano in the same train and who in 1969 published a memoir of Auschwitz entitled *Più morti, più spazio*, testified in a letter dated March 1, 1946, that in early November Roberto and Giorgio were still alive and in reasonable health. Here is the letter in its entirety:

> *Dear Signorina Sonnino, in possession of your valued letter of the 25th of last month, I hasten to communicate to you what I have already had occasion to say to your uncle, who came to see me some months ago. I recall perfectly your whole family and therefore your brothers, with whom I made the journey to Auschwitz. I was with them in Block 14 Lager D, and we worked together for several days unloading freight cars. Then, on November 4, I entered the hospital in Block 14 for an injury to my left leg, the result of a beating. I was operated on and remained in the hospital until the arrival of the Russians. In the hospital, also in November, I saw two of your brothers, who had been admitted for dysentery to the same Block 14. Later, that is, in the month of December, I was moved to Block 12 of the hospital, and after that I didn't see any of your three brothers again. When I saw the two in Block 14 they were not seriously ill, so that one would not have thought they were dying: but too much time and too many events passed after my*

first encounter with them, so that I cannot supply other details that might allow you to get a more precise idea of their fate. However much I search my memory, I can add nothing else definite to what I have already told you. I hope that your stay in Merano is helpful to you and that you may soon regain full health. With my best wishes, please accept my kind regards.

P.S. Although further research may be useless, will you, too, see if you can tell me anything of my wife Signora Elena Segre Saralvo, a thin blonde, ill with diabetes, who arrived with us at Birkenau and who unfortunately disappeared a few days after we entered the lager.

The second brother to die was Roberto, the one described as the strongest and most enterprising. Information about him, though vague, came from Simone Spritmann, in the letter quoted near the end of the diary. Giorgio endured a little longer: the boy who had had panic attacks during the bombardments, and who upon arriving in Auschwitz "was in our mother's lap, curled up as if he had gone back in time, as if he were asking the one who bore him to take him back into herself, to gradually eliminate him, to take away the life she had given him."

The first image of Piera Sonnino after her return is both sad and happy. A row of girls on hospital beds, chatting, on a terrace flooded with sun. "At that time, the treatment for skeletal tuberculosis was sunbaths," recalled Carla Curti, who met Piera in the hospital and found her again, almost fifty years later, through *Diario*. "My eyes fell on the title of the journal, *A Manuscript Recovered. The Deportation of My Family*, by Piera Sonnino. I felt a tug at my heart. Piera Sonnino. Suddenly I found myself again in a room (late May, June, 1948) of the Codivilla Sun Therapy Institute in Cortina," Curti explained to me in a letter, in which she recalled her friend. The day before we had spoken on the telephone.

It was a Wednesday, it's clear in my mind as if it were yesterday. We were on a terrace and she said to me: "What are you doing this evening? Will you come and see me?" We were lying down on the hospital beds. We couldn't get up. Before that moment we had exchanged maybe a couple of words, but I had noticed the tattoo on her arm right away. I recall that she was on the second floor, in the section for rich people, because her aunt and uncle were well off. So that night I had the porter take me to her room—his name was Teofilo, I still remember that. I went into this room, I remember the dim light, a night table on the right with some small photographs that I noticed right away, and also her friend was there. She said to me, "This is Carla, let me introduce my friend." Then, indicating the photographs on the night table: "And this is my family that I don't have anymore. We were six children, my mother and my father; I'm the only one left." That night she told me everything. I didn't know anything about Auschwitz at that time. She did all the talking. For all these years I have always wondered what happened to Piera. I also remember her aunt and uncle from Milan, the little aunt, always dressed in black with a dark hat. Piera said that they were good to her, but later I think they didn't behave so well.

Carla Curti didn't want to tell me what she meant, for fear of betraying Piera's trust. After listening to the story of the death of Bice, Carla asked how she had reacted. Piera responded: "Carla, do you think we had feelings? What sort of feelings would we have? They wanted us not to be human anymore. When Bice died, for a second I thought: I'll eat her potato skins."

———

For five years Sonnino remained in hospitals. She returned to Genoa in September 1950, seven years after the family was arrested. She began to work as a typist and met Antonio Parodi, whom she married in 1954. Through him she became close to the PCI, the Communist Party. Bice, the oldest daughter, explains: "Papà gave a political direction to Mamma's suffering." The aunt and uncle in Milan, who had helped her during her years of convalescence, and who were her last remaining relatives, did not accept their niece's becoming a Communist. And Piera was again alone. But even in the Party, it wasn't all easy. Luciano Degl'Innocenti, a former leader of the Genoese Party, remembered her in the early fifties: "She was a silent woman, a solid member of the Party, but she stayed on the sidelines. She seemed not to want to be noticed. She didn't speak much of what had happened to her, except within her small circle of friends, made up for the most part of Genoese Jews from the Party. It was as if she had cut out a small space for herself."

The proportions of the destruction of the Jews of Europe were not yet known, and the extermination camps were included in the overall figure of 60 million dead in the Second World War.

Degl'Innocenti explained:

> People did not begin to talk about the Holocaust
> until the late fifties. Not even in the Party. People
> talked about the German extermination camps, but
> the victims seemed to have been in equal measure
> Gypsies, Russian soldiers, Communists, and Jews.
> Further, there was the influence of Stalin, who in the
> last years of his life reinforced the elements of anti-
> Semitism that had always existed in Russia and its
> politics. Even within the Communist Party, therefore,
> Jews were seen with distrust if not hostility.

 Degl'Innocenti continued:

> Piera wasn't held up as an icon, because at the time the
> Party did not display icons whose name did not end in
> "off." The two wings of the Party were clashing then,
> the modernist and that of the workers. The Jewish
> doctors' plot to kill Stalin had just been made public,
> and had kindled a violent debate on Judaism. There
> were some who claimed (especially the extremists
> among the workers) that a Jew was good only if he
> was a Communist, otherwise he was an enemy.

 Piera's reaction, yet again, was to stay out of the
way, to remain in the shadows. After Bice was born,

in 1954, she stopped her activities as typist to take care of her daughters (Maria Luisa was born in 1959), of her husband, and, after his death (he died in 1973, at the age of fifty), of his nephews Davide and Francesco. From 1964 to 1968, the Parodi family lived in Budapest, for *l'Unità*. For Piera, who after Bice's death had been the only Italian among seven hundred Hungarian Jews, it was another torment.

Every day for years, accompanying her daughter Bice to school, Sonnino had to meet the daughter and nephew of the woman who had reported her family. Sometimes she murmured almost to herself, pointing out to the child the schoolmate who had behind him the other side of the same story, but she did this with the same moderation, the same restraint in judgment, the same sorrow that distinguishes her whole story. Describing the moment of the arrest, she wrote:

> The person who ordered our arrest was Brenno Grandi, who was acquitted, in a trial in 1947, because he managed to show that he had not been cruel to Jews for his personal gain; but those four agents who carried out his orders, wherever they might be today, I want them to know that the

moment they dragged us from our house, that first and only time they saw us, they started us on our journey toward death. For me today, in my memory, they have the face of death.

These are the strongest, yet most measured, words that can be addressed to another human being.

A year before her death, Sonnino, already ill, had agreed to be interviewed by Chiara Bricarelli for Steven Spielberg's *Survivors of the Shoah*. In the two hours of recording, the pain of remembering, along with the effort to be precise, was so intense that it screened any emotion. But what we learn is identical to what had been written on paper four decades earlier. For Sonnino memory is modest. To preserve the past, to keep it with you until you are able to hand it down to others, is the unique capacity that makes us human.

Piera Sonnino's story is over. In a few minutes the mud of Auschwitz will have dried, and the features of the dead will merge, swallowed up again by the history of a century that has been a long time dying. Now we return to our warm houses.

Afterword

What Went Right In Italy?

Mary Doria Russell, author of
A Thread of Grace

MARY DORIA RUSSELL holds a Ph.D. in anthropology from the University of Michigan. Her novels *The Sparrow* and *Children of God* won nine national and international awards. *A Thread of Grace* was recently nominated for a Pulitzer Prize. All three novels were bestsellers, and today they are studied in colleges and universities in literature and religion courses. Dr. Russell lives in Cleveland, Ohio. Her web site is www.marydoriarussell.info.

On September 8, 1943, General Dwight D. Eisenhower announced that Italy's government had broken with Nazi Germany and made a separate peace with the Allies. Within hours, the Nazi occupation of Italy began. On that day, the Jewish population of Italy is believed to have been about 50,000 souls. Twenty brutal months later, when Germany finally surrendered, approximately 43,000 Jews were still alive in Italy. This means that at least 85 percent of the Jews in Italy survived the Holocaust.

That may be the highest survivor rate in Nazi-occupied Europe where, typically, 90 percent of the

Jewish community in each country was hunted down, rounded up—often with the active participation of the gentile citizens of those occupied nations—and deported to concentration camps to be killed outright or worked to death as slave laborers.

The survival rate in Italy is all the more remarkable because the figure includes thousands of foreign Jews who were hiding in Italy when the Nazi occupation began. In Romania, for example, a high percentage of native-born Jews were saved by their king, but foreign Jews were handed over to the Nazis for deportation and death.

We tend to believe that the Dutch showed remarkable solidarity with their Jewish neighbors because everyone knows about Anne Frank and the handful of Jews hidden with her in the Secret Annex. Yet we often forget that they all were betrayed by somebody who could have kept quiet but chose to turn them in only a few months before the end of the war.

The Danes certainly deserve respect and gratitude for smuggling 7,100 Jews across their country to safety in neutral Sweden, hiding them by day, moving them by night. Every dash across Denmark was a death-defying risk, but to understand Jewish survival in occupied Italy, you must imagine fifty thousand Anne Franks hidden in apartments and houses and barns, in seminaries and convents and monasteries, not for days or weeks but for twenty months of a vicious and vindictive occupation.

For nearly two years, the Gestapo searched door to door, town to town, valley to valley. It was a capital crime if Jews were caught hiding on one's property. The Gestapo offered large cash bounties for Jews, and anyone caught concealing them was publicly executed. But in Italy, neither the bribes nor the intimidation worked.

For sixty years, the world has asked what went wrong in Germany, Austria, Poland and France. Those will always remain important questions, but I believe it's also crucial to understand why things went differently in Italy.

Fascist Italy fought for three years as an ally of Germany and Mussolini imposed anti-Semitic race laws on his nation. Italian Catholics went to Masses with the same type of liturgy as Polish, French, German, and Austrian Catholics and heard the ugly lessons about the Jews as Christ-killers. Why, then, did so many Italians take such risks to protect Jews?

181

I devoted seven years of my life to studying the Italian response to the persecution of Jews in the Second World War and to writing *A Thread of Grace*, a novel that tells the story of the Jewish underground near Genoa during the Nazi occupation, and of the vast network of peasants, priests, and nuns that saved so many Jewish lives in nearby Piemonte. During those seven years of research, I read mountains of histories and memoirs and carried out scores of interviews with elderly survivors. I spoke to farmers, housewives, engineers, architects, Jews, Catholics, Communists. No one could recall a single Jew who was betrayed to the Germans by an Italian; in fact, many sources, published and private, specifically stated that Jews were never turned over.

The novel was published in February 2005 and since then I've received many hundreds of e-mails and spoken to thousands of people, including elderly men and women, Catholics and Jews, who lived through those awful days in Italy and came forward to tell me their stories. None knew of a single Jew who had been betrayed. There were certainly arrests by the Gestapo and captures by the Waffen-SS. There were deportations from Italy and well over six thousand deaths, but if there had been any betrayals, I was unable to uncover them in all that time. I was beginning to believe, provisionally, that I never would.

Then, in May 2006, I received a copy of Piera Sonnino's heartbreaking memoir, and learned for the first time of a betrayal—a betrayal, furthermore, that took place in Genoa in 1944, in the very place and time that I described in *A Thread of Grace*. A family of eight sold out for 50,000 *lire* by a Fascist official. A family of eight blamed by the arresting officer for crucifying the Lord Jesus Christ. "What trouble you've been in since then," he remarks sadly, and sends them off with a sort of mild regret that they had been unwise enough get themselves born Jewish and were perverse enough to stay that way. A family of eight, seven of whom would soon be dead. Of all her family, Piera alone would be numbered among the survivors.

For me the most striking aspect of Piera Sonnino's account is how much help she and her family were in fact offered until the day they were betrayed: "Twice in the following days, we experienced concretely the human solidarity that had supported us; twice, solutions were offered that could have saved our lives." Piera's whole family might well have lived if only they had accepted the hands that reached toward them, but, as she tells us, they were modest, lost, and confused, and her mother wanted them to stay together at all cost.

Consider the story of Miriam Krauss. When I interviewed her in 1998, Signora Krauss was the secretary of the main synagogue of Genoa. She had been a small child during the war and her memories naturally lack some details, but she recalls a night when her family—Austrian Jews in Italy illegally— got off a train in some small northern Italian town. All the houses were dark except one. Desperate to find shelter for her young children, Miriam's mother summoned the nerve to knock on the door. A woman answered. "We were obviously foreign, obviously Jewish," Miriam told me. "The lady started to yell—it was probably something like, 'Get away from here! We've got nothing to do with people like you!' "

Behind her, however, the woman's daughter was writing something down. She handed Frau Krauss a slip of paper and pointed down the street. Miriam's mother realized that they had been offered a solution that might save their lives: an address. She led the children there, and again knocked on a door. They waited while dressing gowns were pulled on and lamps were lit, and this time when the door was opened to them, they were quickly pulled inside.

Twenty minutes later, Miriam recalled, "the lady who yelled" appeared at her neighbor's door with milk for the children and extra blankets for the whole family. She apologized to the Krausses and they were told, "A big Fascist lives across the street from her. She had to make a show for him."

For the rest of the war, "the lady who yelled" looked out for the Krauss family. When one place became too dangerous for them to stay, she arranged to move them somewhere else where they would be safe: to the hills, to a farm, to an abandoned building. Miriam never learned the lady's name. In those days, names were rarely given; if caught, you couldn't reveal what you didn't know.

At the end of the war, the entire Krauss family was still alive because they knocked on that door in the middle of the night. I have no doubt that "the lady who yelled" would have done the same for the Sonnino family.

———————

One of the most important sources for *A Thread of Grace* was Alfred Feldman. On September 8, 1943, Alfred was a Belgian teenager, one of 1,200 Jews who crossed the Maritime Alps from France to Italy with the retreating Italian Fourth Army. For the next twenty months, he and his father were hidden, fed, and defended in the very hills and valleys that Piera Sonnino's family could have fled to.

As Alfred relates in his own memoir, he and his father lived among peasants very much like the one who told Piera that "humanity is not divided between Jews and non-Jews but between those who possess everything and those who possess nothing, between those who work the land and do not enjoy its fruits and those who do not work the land and appropriate for themselves the harvest of field and vineyard."

Piera was right to believe that those words— spoken when her mere presence in the peasant's field was a capital crime—contained a profound truth. At the end of the war, Alfred wrote down the names of thirty-three Italians who sheltered him and his father from the Nazis. There were many others whose names he never learned—like the girl who simply noticed that he looked nervous and created a diversion at a railway checkpoint.

If we estimate that only ten people knew and aided each of the forty-three thousand surviving Jews, that means a minimum of four hundred and thirty thousand Italians were rescuers. The real number is likely much, much higher than that, and many Italians paid for their decency with imprisonment, torture, and death.

The reasons so many foreign and Italian Jews survived in Italy, I believe, are deeply rooted in the particularities of Italian history and culture. Two thousand years ago, the Jewish historian Flavius Josephus believed that about 10 percent of the Roman Empire's overall population was Jewish. (By comparison, modern Jews make up less than 2 percent of the American population.) Josephus estimated that there were ten thousand Jews in Rome alone. The Jewish community is the oldest in Europe, and it flourished under Julius Caesar and Augustus centuries before the Vatican was built.

Josephus tells us that conversion to Judaism among Romans was fairly common, particularly among women who appreciated the ethics and values of Judaism and who wanted to raise their children in that framework even if they were not born to it. Men converted, too, but less often, being understandably reluctant to be circumcised as adults.

For several reasons, Roman authorities were ambivalent about Jewish influence—Jews were atheists by Roman standards because they wouldn't sacrifice to the pantheon of gods that underpinned Roman culture. The idea of the Sabbath was considered dangerously subversive; the notion of a day of rest might promote sloth and indolence among the workers of the Empire. In general, though, Rome was a pretty good place for Jews for about five hundred years, until the Emperor Constantine ended Roman religious tolerance and declared Christianity the state religion. Conversion to Judaism became a crime.

After the fall of the Empire, the Italian peninsula broke up into a dozen or so small warring states. In some places during the next fifteen hundred years,

Italy was the best place in Europe to be Jewish; in other places and other times, it has been the most backward and intolerant. The word *ghetto* was coined in Venice. The Papal States, which stretched across the central third of the peninsula, had an appalling record of anti-Semitism. Yet there have always been Italian cities where Jews were an integral part of the community. One of those times was during the Second World War.

Jews were prominent from the very creation of the modern Italian state. When the American Civil War was being fought to divide North from South, Italy was in the midst of a war against the Papal States to unify the north and south. For centuries, the pope had fielded troops, coined money, and been an active player in European power politics, but by the end of the 1860s, the Papal States were reduced to their present status as Vatican City, and the military power of the pope was gone.

Italian Jews fought with Mazzini, Cavour, and Garibaldi, for the King and a united Italy, and for the liberal ideals of liberty, equality, and justice. When the war for unification was won, Jews had earned full citizenship and were passionately committed to the royal House of Savoia and to the Italian nation.

The closest American analogy might be the modern civic participation of American blacks after distinguishing themselves in combat at the end of the Second World War and in Korea and Vietnam. Despite a dreadful history, American blacks and Italian Jews proved their courage and competence in battle and, after they had done so, any suggestion that they were unworthy of full citizenship became increasingly unacceptable and absurd, both to the minorities themselves and to those who had fought beside them.

After unification, the Italian armed forces became a meritocracy rather than a hereditary career, and since 1870 Jews have been part of the Italian military elite. When the French were railroading Captain Dreyfus and when it was illegal for a Jew to become an officer of the German or Russian armed forces, Italy had Jewish admirals and generals. Both the oldest and the youngest decorated Italian heroes of the First World War were Jews. Jews were highly respected as officers and as enlisted men.

In the decades after unification and before the Second World War, Italian Jews flourished in a country that was often actively Judeophilic. There was a Jewish prime minister and there were Jewish senators and mayors, Jewish jurists, civil servants, doctors, teachers, and engineers. Ordinary Italians have told me that it was considered an honor to have a Jew visit their home, and that Jews have long been admired as an intellectual, political, and professional elite.

In the aftermath of the First World War, Italian Jews joined the Fascist Party in exactly the same percentage as their countrymen—about 10 percent. And they joined for all the same reasons. The devastation of the Great War, the political and social upheavals of the 1920s, and the economic miseries of the 1930s caused people around the world to turn to charismatic political leaders. Italian Jews were no different. They were concerned about the bloody Communist takeover in Russia, which had happened only five years before Mussolini's rise to power in 1922. They craved order after years of strikes and chaos. And they wanted to see a unified Italy join the other nations of Europe as a great power.

Mussolini openly admired Judaism and early in his regime there were Jewish Fascists at the top of his government—fiercely nationalistic Italian Jews, many of them veterans of the Great War. Mussolini himself had many Jewish friends and even a Jewish mistress. His daughter nearly married a Jew when she was young and in that she wasn't alone. In 1938, about half of all Italian Jews were married to Catholics, the same rate of intermarriage among American Jews today. Intermarriage distressed clergy of both religions but, like modern Americans, most Italians saw it as the natural result of shared values and shared lives, and took pride in a religious tolerance and cultural sophistication that was unmatched elsewhere in the world at that time.

In spite of all that, Mussolini crumbled under pressure from Berlin and issued his own anti-Semitic race laws in 1938, amid widespread Italian skepticism about the very existence of "racially pure Italian Aryans." Rome, after all, had conquered the entire Mediterranean basin. The legionnaires usually remained garrisoned in these conquered regions for years. Roman soldiers settled down, married the local girls, and had children. As my father used to say, "Go back far enough, and everybody's a little Italian." Many soldiers brought their families home when their tour of duty was up.

Italy itself has been invaded by just about everyone in Europe and North Africa at one time or another: Carthaginians, Goths, Visigoths, Gauls, Vandals, Spaniards, the French, the Scots, the English, Austrians, Hungarians—with all the ensuing raping and pillaging that conquest generally entails.

Furthermore, the Italian peninsula has the longest warm-water seacoast in Europe. Its ports have been visited by ships from around the known world for thousands of years. (I'm an anthropologist. We like to call the result of sailors' port visits "gene flow.")

Given that history, the anti-Semitic laws were widely understood to be an embarrassing fiction cooked up to appease Hitler and not to be taken seriously. There were many exemptions and a list of ways for Italian Jews to become "Aryanized," in addition to subterfuge and minor bribery or the cooperation of a friend at the registry.

The Italian race laws were without question distressing, insulting, and damaging, but they weren't impossible to work around, which brings me to another of the factors in the Italian response to the Holocaust. For good or ill, Italians are not cowed by authority, and delight in circumventing laws they don't care for. One word from Rome, and everyone does exactly as he pleases. This, too, was a factor during the Nazi occupation, along with another set of emotions: injured pride and real resentment.

Even before the occupation began, the Germans consistently treated their Italian allies with casual contempt. The German high command routinely put Italian troops into impossible strategic positions, as when they were sent to be slaughtered by the Soviets on the eastern front. When the Italians were predictably overwhelmed by superior forces, they were sneered at for being bad soldiers and called militarily incompetent. When the occupation began, the majority of Italian citizens were either actively hostile to Germany or simply had no motive to cooperate with the Germans.

Because of integration and intermarriage, by 1943 even the most observant and religiously serious Italian Jews looked, dressed, sounded, and acted just like everyone else. Except in Rome itself, Italian Jews lived in mixed neighborhoods. Jews and Catholics grew up together and went to school together. They were on the same soccer teams, they worked together, they ate and argued together, they married one another, and continued to argue. When the chips were down, every native-born Italian Jew had Catholic relatives, Catholic friends, Catholic co-workers and neighbors that he or she could rely on. Catholic Italians either knew Jews personally, or knew and admired them as public figures. The ironic truth is that in Italy, integration, assimilation, and intermarriage were not threats to Jewish survival but central to it.

The single exception to this pattern of assimilation was the ghetto of Rome, which had remained a distinct Jewish neighborhood into modern times. There, beneath the windows of the Vatican, Jews had historically been subjected to the Church's most relentless and soul-deadening efforts to convince them of their sinful folly in refusing to convert to Catholicism. It is not surprising that Piera Sonnino's grandparents were from Rome's Jewish community. For generations, Roman Jews had been taught by sad experience the importance of "silence and control of one's feelings" in the face of persecution. These were lessons Piera's mother taught her children, lessons that inculcated "a sort of resignation to our destiny . . . a sort of fatalism" that might have been common among Roman Jews, but not in the rest of the Italian Jewish community.

The largest direct action against Italian Jews took place in Rome early on the morning of Yom Kippur, October 16, 1943, about five weeks after the occupation began. The Nazis ordered Italian policemen to surround the Jewish neighborhood. One thousand one hundred men, women, and children were rounded up and held for a huge ransom in gold. In solidarity with the Jews of Rome, Catholic parishes took up collections of jewelry and donated it to the effort, in the sincere belief that the captives would be freed. Instead, the Gestapo collected the gold, kept it, and deported the captives to the Auschwitz death camp anyway. The best records show that eleven came back. One percent.

In 1943, the existence of the death camps was almost unknown in Italy, where news was tightly censored. Rumors about "factories for killing Jews" were simply too crazy to be believed. Anyone who told of such places would have been regarded with pity as someone whose mind had been unhinged by the ordinary horrors of war. Nevertheless, even without the knowledge that deportation almost certainly meant death for Jews, the Yom Kippur roundup of

196

the Jews of Rome was considered an outrage by Italians all over the country.

———————

One of the people I interviewed for *A Thread of Grace* lives in my own town of South Euclid, Ohio. In 1941, Carmello Furnari was an eighteen-year-old Sicilian draftee, wounded during the Second Battle of the Don on the Russian front. When Carmello returned to Italy in 1943, his home in Sicily was already behind Allied lines. He and a buddy tried twice to get through the front south of Naples, but the fighting was so ferocious that they had to return north to Rome.

Carmello had a cousin in Rome who got him a job working for the Germans as an auxiliary police-man and he was one of the officers who witnessed the Yom Kippur roundup. His voice still shook with outrage more than fifty years later when he told of how the Jews of Rome were treated. He had never even met a Jew before the Yom Kippur roundup, but from then on, whenever he found out that there was going to be a sweep through his police district, he

197

would get up at 4 A.M. and knock on every door to warn the neighborhood. He says that all the police-men of Rome did the same. After that first roundup, the only time Jews were caught was when someone had been out of the neighborhood while the warnings were circulated. Carmello said a man might come home on the bus and walk right into the Gestapo net. But those were accidents, not the result of inaction. Italian police saved thousands of Jews that way.

Later I met an elderly woman who was one of the Romans alerted by the police and she confirmed Carmello's story. She lived in a mixed apartment house and said that when the cops gave a warning, every neighbor would take one piece of furniture from the Jews' apartment and hide one member of the family. When the Gestapo showed up, their apartment would be empty and all the neighbors would play dumb. "Oh, they left. . . . No, I don't know where they went. Were they Jewish? I had no idea! We don't pay attention to things like that."

———

Playing dumb was often a satisfying and effective way of dealing with the Germans, especially before the occupation began. Very few Americans know that, at its high water mark, the Italian army occupied southeastern France, western Yugoslavia, Greece and Salonica and Libya, as well as parts of Russia. What's important is that European Jews knew it, and tens of thousands of them took refuge behind Italian lines because they knew the Italians weren't anti-Semitic, and that they treated Jews like human beings.

Early in the war, Italy's foreign minister Count Luca Pietromarchi declared that, as a matter of national pride and honor, under no circumstances would anyone under the authority of the Italian armed forces be handed over to representatives of another government for any reason.

When confronted by authorities attempting to execute German "Surrender on Demand" orders for the removal of undesirables, Italian officials would become artistically inefficient. They would shuffle through papers and discover that they required another permit, or a stamp, or perhaps a letter from Rome, even to respond to such a request.

There are dozens of Gestapo memoranda expressing intense frustration with Italian intransigence in implementing racial laws, and testimony from none other than Hitler's propaganda minister Joseph Goebbels, who wrote: "The Italians are extremely lax in their treatment of Jews . . . in their occupied territories. . . . They will not permit their being drafted for work or compelled to wear the Star of David. Everywhere, even among our allies, the Jews have friends to help them." That was certainly an overstatement in most of Europe, but it was true of all Italian-occupied territories.

The war was a disaster for Italy, and Mussolini was deposed by Italy's king Vittorio Emmanuele III in July 1943. The king replaced *il Duce* with Field Marshal Badoglio and the new government immediately began secret negotiations with the Allies to make a separate peace. The Allies agreed to wait until September 10 to make the armistice public in order to allow the Italian armed forces to make an orderly retreat from their occupied territories and, not incidentally, to evacuate many thousands of Jews under their protection.

The Badoglio government quietly alerted the Italian Jewish relief organization DELASEM (*Delegazione Assistenza Emigranti Ebrei*) that the armistice was about to take effect. DELASEM passed the word to Jewish refugees behind Italian lines to converge on a number of Mediterranean ports and wait to be evacuated by sea in the boats DELASEM was hiring for that purpose.[*]

For reasons I have never been able to ascertain, General Eisenhower disastrously made the armistice public two days early. Since Mussolini's fall, the German government had expected Italy to surrender and switch sides and had massed troops on the peninsula and on the borders of the Italian territories. The moment the announcement was made, German troops stormed the port cities, capturing tens of thousands of Jews, and promptly deporting them to the death camps, which were operating at full capacity by that time.

The Wehrmacht also had standing orders to execute Italian officers immediately. This decapitated the Italian resistance for almost a year, but ordinary soldiers did not abandon the Jews who had taken

---

[*]   I believe that Piera Sonnino must have been referring to DELASEM when she wrote of an organization that had appeared on September 8 "as if out of nowhere—or perhaps it had already been active" in getting refugees out of danger. Indeed, DELASEM was well known in Genoa, but her family's self-imposed isolation evidently extended even to Genoese Jewish groups.

shelter behind their lines. Many refugees had flocked to the ports, but not all of them got word to do so. Chance, and the Italian army, saved their lives. The soldiers did not succeed in saving every Jew, but they made an extraordinary effort to do precisely that. In the confusion of the first days after the armistice, they believed that the war was over for Italy and that if they could only get the Jews across the border into Italy they would be safe.

Instead, overnight, Italy went from being Germany's ally to an occupied country, another factor in the Italian response to the Holocaust. In other occupied nations, the Nazis were able to divide the population—they could cut Jews out of the herd. They could arrest Communists and gypsies and homosexuals, knowing that most of those who watched were indifferent or actually approved, but this didn't happen in Italy.

Shortly after the armistice, the Wehrmacht began to round up Italian males between the ages of fifteen and sixty for forced labor. Hundreds of thousands were loaded into freight cars and shipped north to work in German factories under the same appalling conditions experienced by all of Hitler's enemies. Soon, everyone in Italy was hiding someone—a father, a brother, a son, a cousin. People will tell you, "Half of Italy was hiding the other half." To hide a Jewish neighbor was no additional risk, and another form of resistance.

Shortly after the occupation began, German commandos parachuted into Mussolini's mountain exile, retrieved him and installed him as the head of a puppet government they named the Republic of Salò. New loyalty oaths were demanded of Fascist officials; army units were reconstituted and given German officers, and career Italian officers found themselves taking orders from German lieutenants decades their junior. German high-handedness steadily eroded any residual willingness to cooperate.

There were also sincere and vicious Fascists who did everything they could to support the German occupiers and who collaborated with the SS in the arrest, torture, and executions of their own neighbors. At the end of the war, in 1945, there were still Italian troops fighting with the Germans, as well as Italian government officials who remained committed Fascists to the end and have remained so to this day.

I never found anyone who admitted to being with the Republic of Salò, or even in Mussolini's earlier government. To escape prosecution, or even summary execution, during the Italian civil war that followed hard on the end of the Second World War, collaborators all claimed that they had secretly helped Jews or the resistance. To hear them tell it, no one in the Italian government or armed forces ever fired a shot in anger—everyone was a partisan.

The veterans I interviewed were decorated members of the armed anti-Fascist resistance, both Jews and Catholics. I don't believe they had any reason to burnish the reputation of their Fascist countrymen, and yet they told stories of Fascist government officials who warned Jews of German sweeps, stole German identity papers, forged official signatures, gave blank ration cards to Jews, or funneled information to the partisans.

My own conclusion was that—regardless of their position on the political spectrum from Communist to Fascist—nearly all Italians were united in their refusal to hand Jews over to the Nazis, with few contemptible exceptions.

Piera Sonnino is unsparing in her disgust for the men who betrayed her family, but she also praises the marvelous conscience of the peasants whose names she never learned but whose silence protected her family in the first months of the occupation. She recounts the repeated efforts of the lawyer Sciarretta to save her family and to give them money. Her brothers Paolo and Roberto found jobs with small businesses in the city—businesses owned by people who knew them before the occupation, who knew they were Jews and employed them anyway, at the risk of their livelihoods and their lives. She tells us of Signora Bancalari, who found the Sonninos a place in Val Trebbia where they could hide, and of the desperately poor people on the neighboring farms who provided polenta and potatoes and chestnut flour that winter. She remembers the *carabiniere* who warned them that silence would not be enough to protect them from German sweeps and urged the family to flee. She records the efforts of Perla Moroni and of Signora Bancalari to find apartments in Genoa where the family could hide.

The goodness and courage of those who helped so many like the Sonninos deserve to be recognized and honored in Italy. It would be unjust to deny them that respect simply because others refuse to admit that their own actions deserve condemnation.

———

One doesn't have to be an elderly Fascist to indulge in self-flattering fantasies. Many enduring questions arise from the Holocaust, but the most critical are: How could this have happened? And what would I have done? From the safety of our living rooms, we identify with the victims or the rescuers, not the perpetrators. We are pleased to believe that we would have hidden Anne Frank, that we would have saved Alfred Feldman, or that we could have persuaded Piera Sonnino and her brothers to run for the mountains.

What we must face is that Adolf Hitler did not spend his life in isolation—he spoke aloud of his hatreds and paranoid delusions, and millions cheered. His malignant narcissism gained him enthusiastic support and the uncoerced hard work of individuals who desired nothing more than to make his repellent dreams a reality, who were delighted to do his thieving and killing for him.

Across Nazi-occupied Europe, hundreds of millions found compelling reasons not to resist the

206

occupation, let alone stick their necks out to help a Jew. The only sensible thing to do was keep your head down, and try not to attract attention. We must never forget the sheer, crazy bravery that any kind of resistance required.

In 1998, I was with Alfred Feldman when he returned to Italy with his entire family. We retraced his steps from the Maritime Alps to Cuneo to Genoa, on the coast, and back up into the valleys and mountains of Piemonte, to Borgo San Dalmazzo and the tiny village of Ritanna. Along the way, we attempted to find every one of the thirty-three people on Alfred's list so I could ask them why they had been willing to help him and his father.

Most of them had died long ago, but there was one woman who still lived in the same house in Ritanna all these years later. Alfred remembered her as "an older married woman with children." Of course, he was a teenager at the time; she was only in her mid-twenties with very small children during the war. When he knocked on her door decades later, an elderly woman came out, stared at him, put her hands on her cheeks and cried, "Alfred!" She immediately called for her granddaughter to come out of the house, saying, "This is Alfred! Remember I told you about how he and his father were in the cave?" The story had become part of the history of the village.

To the very end of the war, German troops continued to scour even tiny towns like Ritanna for Jews. As we traveled through Piemonte and Liguria, Alfred had told us how he and his father had been hidden in the Cave of San Mauro above Ritanna, and we all pictured this as a real cave. Now the old lady pointed. Like her granddaughter, we looked up, and it turned out that the cave was nothing more than a bare indentation in the side of a nearly vertical mountainside. It was just big enough so that Alfred and his father could lie there together like spoons. They had actually been in plain sight if you knew where to look.

The Germans were in Ritanna for forty-eight hours. Each night, one of the boys from the village climbed the mountain with food and water for Alfred and his father. If they had been noticed, everyone in the village would have been herded into the church and it would have been burned to the ground with them in it. The people of Ritanna knew that—it had happened in a town just like theirs, a few kilometers away.

And yet, at the end of her story, what that old woman said was, "Oh, Alfred! We were so frightened for you." Not for themselves. For Alfred. For his father.

When I asked people where they found the courage to take such risks, I heard the same words over and over: "*Era niente.*" It was nothing. Over and over, acts of suicidal bravery or casual courage were dismissed. "I only did what anyone would do." Or, "Anybody with a shred of compassion would have done the same." Or, "I was in a position to help, so naturally I did."

But it wasn't nothing. The ashes of six million Jews, the scarred bodies and souls of millions of others are witness to the fact that what happened in Italy was extraordinary.

Without knowledge of what happened in Italy, any attempt to understand what went wrong in Germany, Austria, Poland, and France is stunted at best and crippled at worst. Piera Sonnino's beautifully written memoir adds significantly to that knowledge.

Italy was not a nation of angels and saints. Nevertheless, it is long past time to honor those little old ladies and crippled old men, who shrug off their own deeds as "nothing." What such people dismiss as "what anyone would have done" is in fact a challenge and a rebuke to all those who could have helped but didn't.

Further Reading

For a historical overview of Jewish survival in occupied Italy, start with:

Meir Michaelis (1978). *Mussolini and the Jews: German-Italian Relations and the Jewish Question in Italy 1922–1945*. Institute for Jewish Affairs / Oxford University Press, London U.K.

Susan Zuccotti (1988). *The Italians and the Holocaust: Persecution, Rescue and Survival*. Lincoln: University of Nebraska Press.

—— (2000). *Under His Very Windows: The Vatican and the Holocaust in Italy*. New Haven, CT: Yale University Press.

For interviews and memoirs:

Nicola Caracciolo, ed. (1986). *Uncertain Refuge: Italy and the Jews during the Holocaust*. Urbana and Chicago: University of Illinois Press.
Interviews with Italian rescuers and refugees.

Ivor Herzer (1989). *The Italian Refuge: Rescue of Jews during the Holocaust.* Papers presented at the National Italian American Foundation Conference at Boston University, November 1986. Washington, D.C.: Catholic University of America Press.
Includes work by Italian and foreign Jews who were rescued by Italian Catholics, as well as political and historical details of the era.

Alexander Stille (1991). *Benevolence and Betrayal: Five Italian Jewish Families Under Fascism.* New York: Summit Books.
The original impetus for *A Thread of Grace;* see especially *The Rabbi, the Priest and the Aviator: A Story of Rescue in Genoa.*

Edda Servi Machlin (1995). *Child of the Ghetto.* Croton-on-Hudson, NY: Giro Press.
Memories of many details of Italian Jewish family life in Tuscany before and during the war. See also: Edda Servi Machlin (1993) *The Classic Cuisine of the Italian Jews I: Traditional Recipes and Menus, and a Memoir of a Vanished Way of Life.* Croton on Hudson, NY: Giro Press.

Kate Cohen (1997). *The Neppi Modona Diaries: Reading Jewish Survival Through My Italian Family*. Hanover, N.H.: University Press of New England.
Written by an American delving into family history.

Silvano Arieti (1981). *The Parnas: a scene from the Holocaust*. Paul Day Books, New York.
The story of a houseful of Jews in Pisa during the war.

Alfred Feldman (2001). *One Step Ahead: A Jewish Fugitive in Hitler's Europe*. Carbondale: Southern Illinois University Press.
Details of the Jewish flight from occupied France to Italy on September 8, 1943; of Piemonte peasant life; and of the welcome given to Jewish refugees.

Harry Burger (1997). *Biancastella: A Jewish Partisan in World War Two*. Niwat: University Press of Colorado.
Memoir of a Jewish refugee who fled to Italy on September 8, 1943, and joined the Italian partisans.

Hermann Wygoda (1998). *In the Shadow of the Swastika*. Urbana and Chicago: University of Illinois Press.

Wygoda was a Polish Jew who fought among the Italian partisans.

Tullio Bruno Bertini (1998). *Trapped in Tuscany: Liberated by the Buffalo Soldiers*. Boston, MA: Dante University Press.

Extraordinarily detailed memoir of childhood in the Italian countryside during the war.

For insight into the peasants and partisans who gave shelter to many Jewish refugees in addition to aiding downed Allied flyers:

Eric Newby (1971). *Love and War in the Appenines*. London: Hodder and Stoughton.

Details of peasant life, relationships between Italian peasants and downed RAF pilots, who received the same kind of welcome as Jewish refugees.

William Pickering (with Alan Hart). 1991 *The Bandits of Cisterna*. London: Leo Cooper.

Details of partisan actions.

Iris Origo (1947). *War in Val D'Orcia 1943–44: A Diary*. Boston, MA: David R Godine.

Walter W. Orebaugh (1994). *The Consul*. Cape Canaveral, FL: Blue Note Books.
The memoir of an American diplomat who joined the Italian partisans, with many observations of the Italian political situation.

Giovanni Pesce (1972). *And No Quarter: An Italian Partisan in World War II*. Ohio University Press. New York translation.
Memoir of urban and rural partisan warfare from the Communist perspective.

Reading Group Guide
for This Has Happened

1. The members of the Sonnino family were all very close. How did their insistence on staying together during their flight help them? How did it hurt them?
2. Why did the Sonnino family keep ending up in Genoa in spite of the clear danger they faced there? How did the chaos of wartime impact the reliability of the information they could gather, their ability to asses the political situation, and ultimately their choices?
3. On numerous occasions the family was geographically very close to people who could save them or to people who would deport them. Discuss the role of chance.
4. How does the family's escape and capture put into relief the gender dynamics among its members? Over the arc of the story, how did these roles change? How would a situation like this play out in a modern family where the roles are not always as clearly defined?
5. The youngest brother, Giorgio, seems at first to be the most fragile and vulnerable, and yet he is the male member of the family who survived longest. Why do you think that is?
6. In the narrative, there is often mention of the merits of blending in, of not attracting attention, both as a traditional bourgeois principle and as a Fascist imposition. How did this influence the Sonnino

family's decisions and what does it tell us about
their values? What does it tell us about the way
concentration camps functioned?

7. How does the fact that the author did not write
   this memoir for publication complicate our experience as readers? How does it affect the way we
   relate to her as an unwitting narrator? Did the fact
   that the book was written as a family record make
   you feel more implicated as a reader?

8. There are some instances where the author vividly
   recalls an image (like her parents in bed the day they
   were deported) and other times in which her mind
   draws a blank or a vague physical rather than visual
   memory. Discuss these instances and the way these
   disjointed memories reflect emotional trauma.

9. In her e-mail to the Italian publisher, Piera
   Sonnino's daughter expressed a certain difficulty in
   deciding to submit her mother's memoir for publication. Why do you think it was a difficult decision
   to make? Why do you think she ultimately decided
   to go ahead and publish it?

10. This is one of very few Holocaust memoirs to come
    from Italy. How does it differ from other Holocaust
    memoirs you've read? How is it similar?